To Have and to Hold

ACHIEVING LIFELONG SEXUAL INTIMACY AND SATISFACTION

ROBERT MOELLER

MULTNOMAH BOOKS · SISTERS, OREGON

TO HAVE AND TO HOLD

published by Multnomah Books
a part of the Questar publishing family

© 1995 by Robert Moeller

International Standard Book Number: 0-88070-679-1

Cover photo © 1994 by The Stock Market,
New York, New York; R.B. Studio, 1993

Cover design by Multnomah Graphics

Printed in the United States of America

Scripture quotations are from:
The Holy Bible, New International Version (NIV)
© 1973, 1984 by International Bible Society,
used by permission of Zondervan Publishing House

For information:
QUESTAR PUBLISHERS, INC.
POST OFFICE BOX 1720
SISTERS, OREGON 97759

95 96 97 98 99 00 01 02 — 10 9 8 7 6 5 4 3 2 1

To Cheryl

"A wife of noble character who can find?
She is worth far more than rubies.
Her husband has full confidence in her and
lacks nothing of value.
She brings him good, not harm, all the days of her life."

PROVERBS 31:10–12

CONTENTS

Preface 8

PART 1: CREATIVE BONDING: ESTABLISHING A HEALTHY SEXUAL RELATIONSHIP

1. Who's Having the Best Sex Anyhow? 13
2. Love Isn't Made; It's Given 25
3. Good Sex Begins in the Bible 41
4. Aren't My Needs Your Needs? 57

PART 2: SUSTAINED PLEASURE: PRESERVING THE SATISFACTION OF MARRIED SEX

5. Time Will Let You 77
6. Keep the Grease Pit Drained 93
7. What You Do When No One Is Watching 107
8. Divorce Is the Problem, Not the Solution 129

PART 3: YOU DON'T SEND ME FLOWERS ANYMORE: RESTORING THE PASSION

9. How to Reconnect a Disconnected Sex Life 143
10. The Trial Was an Error: The Anticlimax of Premarital Sex . 159
11. Recovering from Visual Adultery 177
12. Can You Heal a Broken Heart? 199
13. A Modest Proposal to Rekindle Your Love Life 215

Notes 221

Preface

To Have and to Hold deals with some of the most intimate and sacred aspects of our lives. For that reason it was prudent and necessary to alter the identities, circumstances, and other details of stories that concern individuals and marriages. Unless an individual's first and last name are given, the true identity has been disguised. In many cases the stories and illustrations are a composite of several people or couples.

It is not a book about sexual technique or physiology, nor does it address every problem a couple may experience in their life of intimacy. Instead, it seeks to address the more important questions of the attitudes of our heart and to convey the wisdom, superiority, and practicality of God's design for married sexual intimacy.

My objective is to encourage those contemplating marriage to establish their future marriage on the firm ground of God's wisdom, to reassure those who are married that their spouse is their best hope for finding sexual fulfillment, and to point the way toward healing for those who have stepped outside the divine plan for sex and have suffered the consequences.

Finally, it is my hope the book will help all of us realize the wisdom, happiness, and satisfaction that can be ours from following the simple advice of Proverbs: "Above all else, guard your heart, for it is the wellspring of life."

Acknowledgments

I wish to say thank you to the following individuals and organizations for their contributions to this book:

To my wife Cheryl, who helped at every stage of the project from proposal to final editing;

To Carol Bartley, who once again demonstrated her giftedness as an editor and consultant;

To the people of Questar, in particular Don Jacobson and Rod Morris, who embraced the idea of this book with enthusiasm and commitment;

To Phil and Adora Hinerman, who for over three decades in my home church modeled for my generation what a loving and committed marriage relationship looks like;

To Greg Scharf and Marilyn Hiebeler, who took time from their busy lives to read the manuscript and offer extremely valuable advice;

To the staff at Fort Wilderness and Timberlee Christian Center in Wisconsin, who gave me the gifts of time and solitude to work on the manuscript in the spectacular summer beauty of the North;

To Kevin Miller, Marshall Shelley, and the editorial staff at *Leadership Journal* and *Marriage Partnership*, a marvelous group of writers and editors who granted me permission to use material from their consistently fine publications;

To Robert T. Michael, John H. Gagnon, Edward O. Laumann, and Gina Kolata, for their monumental study entitled "Sex in America" (1994);

To all the host churches and participants in our marriage seminars, for sharing their life experiences and wisdom in building strong marriages;

Finally, my thanks to our family—Homer and Inez, Roy and Gladys, Carol, Cinda, Bob and Marilyn, Glen and Carolyn, Chuck and Mary, Cathy, and John and Lori, and all our friends who have offered unwavering love and support for our common vision of strengthening homes and healing marriages. We simply could not have persevered without you.

PART ONE

CREATIVE BONDING: ESTABLISHING A HEALTHY SEXUAL RELATIONSHIP

WHO'S HAVING THE BEST SEX ANYHOW?

A re you married?" he asks.

"No," the young woman replies.

"Are you getting enough sex?"

"Of course. I have four to five men a week."

"Would you like to have sex with that man standing over there?"

"He does look kind of cute. Yeah, I think so."

"Let's go meet him," says the comedian.

"Why not?" she agrees with a smile.

It's late-night television, and Jay Leno directs a young woman, whom he is interviewing at random, to a rugged, good-looking, young guy who is hanging out with friends across the street. Leno leaves the studio to go "live" on the street and record people's reaction to the question, "Are you having enough sex?"

The portable video camera jostles along on the shoulders of the camera crew following him and his guest as they dodge cars, amidst blaring horns, to meet the group of unsuspecting guys.

"Hi, I'm Jay Leno, and this young woman would like to have sex with you," he introduces himself.

Somewhat surprised but not wanting to lose his cool, the young man looks her over and says, "Sure, why not?"

"I'll leave you two alone," Leno smirks, a closeup of his face filling the camera. Back in the studio the audience cheers.

Change the channel—to a popular sitcom about a contentious husband and wife in their late thirties. The frustrated dad is following his son around the house yelling orders, but the boy just ignores him.

"Why won't Billy ever do what I say?" he complains.

"Don't worry about it. He's not yours," quips the wife.

He's left with a stunned expression while she goes back to making pizza. The laugh track goes wild, and so do their ratings.

OUR LAST CHANCE FOR GOOD SEX?

If you were to continue channel surfing, you would probably find a remarkable number of programs with similar situations. Young, noticeably single men and women go from one steamy, intense, often unplanned, sexual encounter to another. The passion, the shapely bodies, the warm California sun—all add up to a continual sexual heaven on earth.

Press the remote control one more time, and you find tired, irritable, noticeably married couples arguing, firing witty and incisive cruise missiles across the room at each other. You see them jostling in the kitchen, tossing zingers in the living room, and sometimes verbally duking it out in public. But one place you'll rarely find them is in bed. Television sends the message loud and clear that sex is for singles, and monotony is for marrieds. Often the only bond that seems to keep these unhappy, unfortunate middle-aged spouses together is their mutual anger, dark humor, and the few obnoxious teenagers who appear on camera occasionally to boast of their own sexual conquests.

It doesn't take A. C. Nielsen to explain what's happening on television. When it comes to portraying sex, the message is clear: the single life is your last chance for a good time. To be young and unmarried means a banquet table of sexual gourmet delights, exquisitely packaged, simply yours for the taking. No commitments, no hassles, no long-term troubling relationships.

But to be married? On television it's the equivalent of taking a vow of celibacy. It's a bread-and-water existence of stale partners, lifeless relationships, and lukewarm romantic leftovers. The only remote possibility for any sexual excitement for the aged (over twenty-one) is to have an affair (an "act of courage" as one program called it). Otherwise, matrimony and monogamy are the staples of a malnutritious diet that eventually leads to complete sexual starvation.

A STARTLING STUDY

But is this prime time picture of who's hot and who's not really accurate? Are the young, the restless, and the beautiful really participating in nonstop, world-class, sexual Olympics? And is the older, married crowd locked out of the stadium with no hope of getting tickets to the main event?

Is everyone having a good time except married people?

The answer is a resounding no.

At least that's what a team of professional researchers at the University of Chicago concluded in 1994. After launching the most comprehensive survey of the sexual behaviors of Americans ever conducted, using the latest in scientifically controlled survey techniques, they came to a set of startling and profound conclusions:

America has a message about sex, and that message is none too subtle. Anyone who watches a movie, reads a magazine, or turns on the television has seen it. It says that almost everyone but you is having endless, fascinating varied sex.... We tell ourselves that marriage may be a necessary social institution but that it is deadly to a sex life. If you want to have a lot of sex with a partner, you must be unattached, on the loose, ready to seize opportunities when they come your way. We tell ourselves that everybody is having lots of sex, and that those who are not are probably frustrated and miserable.... All those beliefs, suspicions, and tales are wrong.[1]

What do you mean "wrong"?

What the researchers mean is that they're false, fabricated. They are the product of some screenwriter's imagination at some seaside home north of Los Angeles, not the stuff of everyday life in America.

TOO OLD TO ENJOY LOVE?

Let's start with the notion that everyone else but you is having a great deal of sex, particularly if you are so unfortunate as to be married. According to the University of Chicago survey, only one-third of the American public ages eighteen to fifty-nine is having sex two or more times a week. That means the rest of the adult population—the other two-thirds of the American public—is having it only a few times a month or less, or not at all.[2] If you find yourself in that upper one-third of Americans, give your spouse a high five when he or she comes home tonight.

What about the idea that sex is exclusively for the young? Of men and women ages eighteen to twenty-four, 40 percent of the men and 41 percent of the women report having sex two or more times a week. Remember, that's the hot set according to Hollywood. That's the *90210* and *Melrose Place* crowd, where the parties never end and the sheets are never cold.

So what happens as we move up the age ladder, say to ages twenty-four to twenty-nine, the point when demographers tell us the majority of young adults are now married? Party's over, right? After all, what could possibly be more deadly to peak sexual performance than being restricted to one married lover?

Well, say the researchers, the number of men who report having sex two or more times a week jumps to 47 percent, and the same statistic applies to women.

But surely when a person reaches thirty to thirty-nine the sexual drive and frequency must drop like a brick. I mean, this is twenty years out of high school in some cases. The letter jacket doesn't button anymore, and plant life starts to thin on a man's head. A woman is likely to have had children and worn herself ragged keeping everything together.

Actually, frequency does decrease somewhat among this age group, going back to the same level that eighteen- to twenty-four-year-olds enjoy! A remarkable 39 percent of both older men and women report having sex two or more times a week.

So much for the myth that only the young are having fun.

IS MARRIAGE HAZARDOUS TO SEX?

But what of the married people? Won't too many years of paying bills, getting up at six o'clock for work, and hauling kids to doctors and soccer practice put an already waning sex life on the critical list? Isn't marriage the sexual equivalent of passive euthanasia for your love life?

That's not what the researchers found.

Only 26 percent of single, noncohabiting men and 20 percent of single, noncohabiting women are having sex twice a week or more. Compare that to the 43 percent of married men and the 39 percent of married women who enjoy sexual intimacy twice a week or more.

According to the research, cohabiting, nonmarried men and women report the highest frequency of sex during the last twelve months (56 percent of each gender reported having sex twice a week or more). However, these relationships are usually temporary, resulting either in marriage or in changing to new partners. To compare these statistics fairly, the researchers should have compared the frequency of sex between newly married couples with nonmarried, cohabiting couples. My guess is that the sexual activity for newly married couples would be equal to or higher than that of the other couples.

If the conclusions of the study are to be believed, you stand a far better chance of frequent, enjoyable, and consistent sex if you are married than if you are single.

Even as a recently married man in my twenties, I knew that. That's why when a rowdy teenage boy in my youth group once tried to tell me I didn't understand what real sex was about (and apparently he believed he did), I couldn't resist the opportunity. I looked straight at him and said, "Jimmy, your fantasy is my continual reality." I wish you could have seen the look on his face. And I wasn't bragging; I just wanted him to realize that God's plan for sex in marriage was far beyond what he had imagined (or had experimented with). But somehow we've bought the idea that good sex and lifelong marriage can't coexist any better than Nancy Kerrigan and Tonya Harding can figure skate together. It isn't true. Marriage enhances your sex life; it doesn't ruin it.

As the Chicago researchers say, "Those people who are supposed to be having the most sexual intercourse are having it less often than those who are supposed to be having intercourse the least.... The group that has most sex is not the young and footloose but the married."[3]

"Okay," some singles living in the fast lane might argue, "maybe older, married people are getting some loving once in a while. But it can't be as good as what we're enjoying. After all, we, the MTV crowd, are experiencing ultimate sex if anyone is."

I'm afraid I have bad news for this group.

According to the University of Chicago the quality of sex the single person and the married person are experiencing are very different. In fact, they aren't even close. While only 62 percent of single, noncohabiting women report usually or always experiencing climax during sexual intercourse, an incredible 75 percent of married women report doing so.

DO CHRISTIANS HATE SEX?

All right. So maybe older people do enjoy sex. Maybe they do have it as often or more often than many young adults. Maybe they do report a significantly higher level of sexual satisfaction. But certainly if you want to put the nail on the coffin of a couple's love life, all you have to do is introduce religion—something like Christianity, and in the worst case scenario, conservative Christianity. "After all," someone heavily influenced by the media might argue, "who are the modern Puritans among us, the inhibited prudes, the repressed eunuchs, if not the religious conservatives? I mean, these people hate sex. They're joyless, uptight, neurotic people ashamed of their bodies and sexual drives. Right?"

If you measure sexual enjoyment by the standard of always experiencing orgasm when engaging in sexual relations, the one group that stands out is Conservative Protestant women—by a margin of at least 5 percentage points. They are followed close behind by Mainline Protestant and Catholic women, with non-religious women finishing last (10 percentage points behind Conservative Protestant women).[4] For someone whose world-view has been shaped by Ricki Lake, Oprah Winfrey, and Sally Jessy Raphael, these statistics are incredible. How could older, married, religious men and women possibly be enjoying their sexuality more than any other group in society?

The answer lies in the wisdom of the Word of God. As believers these statistics shouldn't surprise us. They're consistent with what the Scriptures say about God's plan for the expression of our sexuality. God designed sex to work best in the context of a lifelong, exclusive, monogamous, committed relationship he calls marriage.

Imagine that you own an Apple Computer. You are having trouble programming it, so you call the 800 number for technical support. Four hours later your front doorbell rings. You open it, and there stands the president of the company. He informs you he's just flown in from the West Coast and wants to help you get your computer on-line. He sits down, and with a few deft keystrokes and commands the computer is suddenly on-line and functioning flawlessly. Now that's tech support!

Believe it or not, God has done exactly the same thing in his Word when it comes to our sexuality. He knows exactly how we're designed and how we're programmed. He knows which instructions, if followed, will produce the most satisfying results.

That's why I believe that the best sex—the most frequent, the most consistent, and the most satisfying—is to be found with the same, lifetime partner in a marriage relationship that has Christ at the center.

The summary statement of the researchers at the University of Chicago acknowledges this possibility: "Our results *could* be read to mean that an orthodox view of romance, courtship, and sexuality—your mom's view perhaps—is the only route to happiness and sexual satisfaction"[5] (italics mine).

THERE'S HOPE FOR ALL OF US

So if finding just one partner, entering into the lifelong commitment of marriage, and making God the centerpiece of our relationship is the best opportunity to find lasting and meaningful sexual satisfaction, where do we begin? And what do we do if we've experienced disappointment or failure along the way? What if our sexual relationship is often more sorrow than ecstasy, more frustration than celebration?

That's why *To Have and to Hold* can offer hope. It can help you discover and implement God's plan for your sexual happiness in the context of marriage. It can assist you in creating, preserving, and redeeming your sexual relationship in order to enjoy all that God intends for both of you. It shows the sobering truth that if you experiment with any other plan for expressing your sexuality, the one thing you seek—sexual satisfaction and love—is the one thing you will destroy.

Ultimately, this book is to help you experience intimate love in your marriage. I'm convinced when all is said and done, love is the deepest need of the human heart. It's the one thing we all seek, we all long for, and that we're all afraid we'll never find. I've never met anyone living a sexually confusing, frustrating, or promiscuous life who wasn't really looking for love.

The reality is that God created us for love, and our sexuality is simply one powerful and beautiful means of expressing this most basic human need. It's not the only way to experience love, but in the context of marriage, it's a central part of the plan. It adds true beauty and meaning to our lives as married couples.

Or as Garrison Keillor observes in his essay "It's Good Old Monogamy that's Really Sexy": "It is almost worth all the misery of dealing with real estate people, bankers, lawyers and contractors—to have a home that has a bedroom where the two of you can go and sometimes do this. It is worth growing up and becoming middle-aged to be able to enjoy it utterly."[6]

But sexual love can never be sustained apart from the other expressions of love in a marriage. It must be part of a total lifestyle that includes understanding the needs of our husbands or wives, choosing to forgive, living unselfish lives, and surrendering ourselves to one another. Sexual love in marriage is simply one instrument in an entire orchestra, which if isolated from the others, can never perform the full symphony God intended.

And perhaps most important of all, sex must be expressed as an act of love and obedience to God. Sexual love in marriage only makes sense when we understand that God designed sex to mirror spiritual oneness. It is similar to the oneness we can experience in our relationship with Christ.

WHAT DR. RUTH WON'T TELL YOU

To Have and to Hold shares insights, principles, and instructions for sexual fulfillment and contentment you won't find on late-night talk shows or sitcoms. They won't be in the women's magazines at the checkout counter, nor will you be likely to find them in Dr. Ruth's syndicated column.

That's because the popular advice and wisdom on how to find sexual fulfillment have been seriously flawed. To quote the researchers from the University of Chicago: "We have found the public image of sex in America bears virtually no relationship to the truth. The public image consists of myths, and they are not harmless.... The resulting false expectations can badly affect self-esteem, marriages, relationships, even physical health."[7]

Some people still can't accept the fact that what we've been told in our culture about sex could be so far from reality. Erma Bombeck jibed, "Having read the latest sex survey that makes us all sound like a 1960 Doris Day movie, I suggest we do a survey on how many people tell the truth on these questionnaires."[8] I draw a different conclusion than Bombeck does. Rather than suspecting the research data isn't true, I suggest that the false notions about sexual love and fulfillment have contributed to the high rates of divorce, damaging infidelity, and tragic, unwanted pregnancies.

But if myths can harm and enslave us, then truth can liberate our lives. My desire is to see spouses and marriages set free. I want to see husbands and wives enjoy one of God's most powerful and wonderful gifts. As the writer of Proverbs says so beautifully, "May you rejoice in the wife of your youth. A loving doe, a graceful deer—may her breasts satisfy you always, may you ever be captivated by her love" (Proverbs 5:18–19).

To see sexual love heal and strengthen our marriage relationships rather than damage and destroy them, we must substitute true wisdom and biblical advice for popular falsehoods and cultural distortions.

Let's begin the process.

Chapter Two

LOVE ISN'T MADE; IT'S GIVEN

It was a warm, sultry July evening. Dennis and Nancy were exhausted from what had been a perfect day and—a perfect wedding. After what seemed like years of planning menus, choosing china, and arranging for out-of-town guests, the ceremony and reception had at last arrived and gone off flawlessly.

Now, here they were—just the two of them, alone in an elegant hotel. This was the moment they had both waited for and longed for. Soon they could consummate their love for each other.

It was all so perfect.

"Honey, I'm waiting for you," said Dennis.

"Just a minute, sweetheart," came the loving reply from the bathroom where Nancy was changing.

"Listen, I'll go get some ice," said Dennis. "The machine is just down the hallway. We passed it when we got off the elevator."

"Okay, honey," came Nancy's voice through the door. "I'll be waiting for you when you get back."

"Whoa," thought Dennis. He walked over to the dresser, where the ice bucket sat, and glanced in the mirror. "You're really a handsome guy," he mused. "And a lucky one."

He had taken off his tuxedo, so now he stood in just his black socks, striped boxer shorts, and white dress shirt. "I don't need to get dressed just to get ice," he thought. "I can sneak out and back in before anyone sees me." He cracked the door and peered down the plush carpeted hallway between the deluxe suites. The hallway was empty. As he opened the door and tiptoed out, ice bucket in hand, he heard the door swing shut behind him and lock.

"Great. The place is deserted," he thought. He strode down the hallway with an air of confidence and mission. He stuck the plastic ice bucket under the nozzle of the machine and pushed the button. A roaring, grinding sound—like gears stuck on a dump truck—filled the tiny enclave where he stood. A moment later ice cubes came crashing out of the spout. He let go of the button as the cubes started to spill over the container.

"Now back to my room. Back to Nancy. Yes."

Dennis took one more look down the hallway to be certain the coast was clear, then headed back to his room in double time. His head nearly swirled with anticipation of what was to come.

Halfway down the hall he froze in his tracks. "Oh, no! I didn't bring my key." Then in his panic he forgot which room was theirs. Was it 315 or 325? Maybe it was 352. "Oh, Nancy, where are you?"

As his mind went blank, a sense of dread poured into Dennis like molten lead. "There must be fifty rooms in this wing," he realized. "I can't start knocking on doors and say, 'Hi, I'm Dennis, and I'm on my honeymoon. Is my bride in there?'"

Just then he heard people getting off the elevator. He bolted for the enclave with the ice machine and hid behind it like a twelve-year-old boy playing hide-and-seek. The voices got closer and closer, then turned into a room just before they reached his spot.

"Whew. That was close. Steady now. Take a deep breath," he counseled himself. "You've got to remember which room you're in." But try as he might to recall his suite, all the doors and rooms looked exactly alike.

Dennis waited for several minutes, weighing his options. None were good. His hopes for his honeymoon were melting as quickly as the ice cubes. It wouldn't do any good to start shouting. Nancy was probably still shut in the bathroom and wouldn't hear him. Besides, that would only arouse attention. Time was running out. It would only be a matter of minutes until someone else came to get ice or a cold soda.

That's when he made his decision. "I've waited years for this night," he thought. "Sometimes a man has to do what a man has to do."

Stoically, bucket in hand, he marched out into the hallway and headed toward a metal door—the door that led to the stairs that led to the lobby. Given other circumstances he might have been less bold, but Nancy was waiting for him. The fragrance of her perfume drove him on like a bull headed out to fresh pasture in the spring.

With a determined attitude Dennis emerged from a side door of the lobby and charted a course bearing 0.90 for the front desk. As he marched through the large reception area with ice bucket in hand and eyes fixed straight ahead, conversations suddenly grew silent. Couples decked in black tuxedos and evening gowns pointed discreetly in his direction.

Dennis refused eye contact. He thought he heard a giggle.

"Excuse me," Dennis said as he approached the front desk.

An attendant in a pressed uniform looked up from his computer screen. "Yes?" he queried, raising an eyebrow.

"You'll have to excuse me. I'm on my honeymoon.... What I mean is I'm registered here.... You see, I've forgotten which room we're in. I'm wondering if you could tell me."

Fortunately the hotel attendant recognized Dennis. He had checked in him and his new bride only an hour earlier. The attendant started to say something, then thought better of it. He handed Dennis a second key and wished him well. Dennis could hear the snickering behind him as he stepped into the elevator. At last he was headed for Nancy, who was sitting alone on the bed, dressed in an elegant negligee, wondering where in the world her new husband was.

It's possible your honeymoon, like Dennis and Nancy's, didn't fulfill your every fantasy or expectation. Best-selling authors Bill and Lynne Hybels said in *Fit to Be Tied* if the memoirs of their honeymoon were ever printed, they would be entitled, "We Flopped in Florida."

One couple scheduled their first night together at a hotel almost four hours from the church where they had been married. They stayed late at the reception, paused for one last round of pictures, and then drove off at twilight. Hour after hour they cruised down the interstate in search of their hotel. The groom was so sexually frustrated by the seemingly endless cross-country trip that tears started running down his cheeks. His wife didn't know whether to laugh or cry with him.

DIRECTION IS DESTINY

Even if your honeymoon had its flaws, what are the positive attitudes and values you can adopt in order to get your sexual relationship back on the right foot?

I want to give love, not make love.

I realize the popular euphemism for sexual intercourse is "making love," but I've always been somewhat baffled by the term. How do you "make" something that can only be given?

Making love sounds too much like the mere mechanical joining of a male and a female body. Giving love sounds much more like the sharing of your soul, your affection, your respect, your deepest concern, and your heart with another person.

Years ago the popular rock group the Rolling Stones had a hit song entitled "I Can't Get No Satisfaction." Mick Jagger sounded angry as he repeated over and over, "I can't get no...I can't get no...I can't get no...satisfaction. But I try, and I try, and I try!" The sexual connotations of the lyrics were obvious.

That's the attitude of far too many of us as we enter married life. When it comes to sex, we are out to get something, not give something. The result may be passionate and frenzied lovemaking for a season, but the inevitable result of emphasizing getting rather than giving is disappointment, loss of interest, and finally frustration.

A husband who enters marriage focused primarily on getting his needs met will be impatient. With his biological makeup he is prone to quick arousal and quick satisfaction. He will be tempted to demand sex on a moment's notice. (There's something to be said for spontaneity—a great deal actually—but showing consideration for our spouse is crucial.)

Assuming his wife experiences sexual arousal exactly the same way, he suggests they have sex right now, fifteen minutes before they're to leave for dinner. If his wife responds without enthusiasm, he's not only hurt but angry. What? Isn't she interested in him anymore? Selfish impatience has set the stage for one of their major arguments.

On the other hand, if a wife doesn't understand the male's need to feel respected, she may wound him by acting bored or uninterested. It may be her way of telling him he isn't taking time to bring her along with him sexually, that she would like more romance or foreplay. But in his mind she has just stamped the word "INADEQUATE" across a huge poster of his face.

That's what's wrong with trying to get what you want instead of trying to give what the other person needs.

Giving love should become a way of life in your marriage that spreads over into numerous areas. For a wife it may mean spending an afternoon helping him work on the car, just to be together. For a husband it may mean walking through a mall as she looks at clothes. It means doing the dishes so your spouse may sit down after a tiring day. It means planning his or her birthday party. It means holding your tongue when you want to say something hurtful or demeaning. It means visiting your spouse's relatives. It means affirming your love each day with words and actions.

Imagine applying the following definitions of "giving love" to your sexual relationship: "Love is patient, love is kind. It does not envy, it does not boast, it is not proud. It is not rude, it is not self-seeking, it is not easily angered, it keeps no record of wrongs. Love does not delight in evil but rejoices with the truth. It always protects, always trusts, always hopes, always perseveres" (1 Corinthians 13:4-7). That type of "giving love" will improve and enhance the quality of your love life in ways that will be hard to imagine.

A professor of mine in seminary told an unforgettable story. His grandfather, who was well into his eighties, discovered he was suffering from prostate cancer. After careful evaluation the doctors determined he would need surgery to remove the malignant tumor. The price of the procedure would be high, however. They warned him he would most likely suffer sexual dysfunction and impotency as a result. He and his wife made a difficult decision.

The professor went into the room shortly after his grandfather woke up from the procedure. Standing by his grandfather's side was his wife of over sixty years. She held his hand as the two of them wept. "It was a sacred moment to watch," the professor told us. "They were grieving the loss of something that had been very special to them through all those decades."

That's why giving love is more important than making love. "Giving love" is an attitude of the heart that says, "I find real joy in seeking the best for you." Even if we someday reach the point where we are no longer able to function sexually, giving and receiving genuine love can still be very much a part of our marriages.

My body now belongs to you.

Recently I had the joy of watching *Shadowlands*, the story of the amazing love affair and marriage of C. S. Lewis, the great Christian writer, and Joy Davidson, a converted Communist. When the two of them were married in Joy's hospital room, the minister had them recite the traditional Anglican wedding vows. One line in particular jumped out at me: "With my body, I thee worship."

At first it sounded overdone, almost idolatrous. I can see admiring or even adoring another person, but worshiping? Really.

Actually the term *worship* means "to ascribe worth or value" to someone. In that sense the old Anglicans might have been on to something, particularly when it comes to our love lives. It is with my body, in the loving act of sexual intimacy, that I communicate how much I value my spouse.

From day one of our marriage we need to view our own bodies as a means of ascribing worth to our husband or wife. In this sense there is no higher valuing than saying, "This body now belongs to you as well as to me. I give it to you in love in order to meet your physical needs and to express the oneness we have pledged ourselves to."

The Apostle Paul put it this way, "The husband should fulfill his marital duty to his wife, and likewise the wife to her husband. The wife's body does not belong to her alone but also to her husband. In the same way, the husband's body does not belong to him alone but also to his wife. Do not deprive each other except by mutual consent and for a time, so that you may devote yourselves to prayer. Then come together again so that Satan will not tempt you because of your lack of self-control" (1 Corinthians. 7:3–5).

Paul was saying we need to be willing to share our bodies with our partners on a regular, frequent basis. Each of us has legitimate sexual needs. God's plan to meet those needs is through our spouses. In fact, it's our "duty" to do so. (I can hear some of you saying, "If that's my duty, put me down for overtime.")

That's why it's so important that couples not use access to their bodies as a means of controlling or manipulating their spouses. In its more extreme form, it's sexual blackmail. It's saying, "Don't touch me until you apologize for what you said in front of your friends," or "Until you lose weight, I'm not interested," or "Until you get a better job and do something with your life, don't come near me."

Paul warns that withholding sex from a mate gives Satan a chance to tempt one or both partners. The stage is then set to think about getting our sexual needs met with another person. More than one affair has resulted from a spouse putting up an emotional "No Trespassing" sign on his or her side of the bed.

A more subtle temptation is to use sex as a weapon and means of control. While we may not go out and commit adultery to release our sexual frustrations, we may turn a source of joy and love into an instrument of punishment and control.

Early in a marriage both the husband and wife need to commit themselves to being available to each other on a consistent, regular basis. While illness and travel can interrupt our sexual relationship, those hiatuses should be temporary at best. If our partners express a desire to make love, we should make every effort to respond in a positive way.

While we can't demand sex from one another, and while we ought to show sensitivity to each other's moods and physical condition, there's nothing wrong with our mates asking for sex. Consider it a compliment. It is an act of valuing us. It is a legitimate marital request. In response we ought to do everything in our power to meet that request even if it means overriding our selfish, cranky temperament at the moment.

Jokes about spouses withholding sex from each other are common, but in the end they're no laughing matter. When we withhold sex, we send a damaging, demeaning, and divisive message to our husband or wife: "You don't deserve me."

Paul tells us, "Therefore honor God with your body" (1 Corinthians 6:20). By living obedient and sexually pure lives, we ascribe honor to our Father in heaven. But in the marriage relationship we ascribe "honor" or "worthship" to our spouses by engaging in sexual intimacy with them on a regular basis.

I want to learn what pleases you.

As married couples we face a fundamental decision each and every time we engage in sexual intimacy: Am I here to please me or you? The answer to that question alone will determine a great deal of our future sexual happiness and fulfillment.

I remember reading in college about an economist from a previous century who believed that if everyone acted in his or her own selfish interest, everyone would benefit.

Let me ask a few fundamental questions in response to this novel theory of life.

Have you ever been in a stadium parking lot when all sixty thousand fans were trying to leave at once? Everyone there is acting in his own selfish interest, so theoretically the lot should clear in record time. But that's not what happens. Unless someone is willing to let the other person go out first, you can be stuck there until next spring.

Or let's say you go out to supper with friends. It's just the four of you. When the server puts the rolls on the table, you all lunge for them, grabbing and snatching the ones you like most. When the server asks for your order, all four of you begin talking, even shouting at the person, at the same time. When the check is finally delivered, everyone refuses to pick it up. Now again, each of you has been acting in his selfish interest, so it ought to be a night to remember. Actually it does turn out that way as all four of you are arrested for check bolting.

Now let's apply this theory to our love life. Again let's assume our economist friend is right—that selfishness benefits everyone. Some modern marriage and sex therapists advocate each partner approaching sex with a selfish perspective. If both people concentrate on pleasing themselves, everyone will go away satisfied they say.

Suppose each of us insists on being the first one to experience sexual climax. If the me-first theory is right, theoretically we should have the most exquisite night of lovemaking ever imagined. In reality one of us may end up satisfied, but the other will find himself or herself extremely frustrated. Hostility, resentment, and distance will soon follow.

Or if each of us insists on having sex only when we are in the mood and in the time and place that suits us best, what will be the result? Eventually neither of us may remember when we last had sex.

Whoever thought that pursuing our own selfish interests would lead to happiness for all has never stood in a crowded line at a McDonald's at lunch hour. Nor do they understand what it takes to produce an intimate and satisfying sex life with a spouse.

Again, the Apostle Paul offers advice we'd do well to apply to our sexual relationship with our spouses. Although Paul was speaking to the church in general on the topic of relationships, the principle applies to our lives of intimacy as well: "Do nothing out of selfish ambition or vain conceit, but in humility consider others better than yourselves. Each of you should look not only to your own interests, but also to the interests of others" (Philippians 2:3–4).

"It takes time to get it right," a newly married husband said to me. He spoke more truth than he realized. Couples don't automatically learn how to please each other sexually. That's part of the discovery process. The important thing is for each of us to commit to learning how to please the other person. Men may need to learn the value of tender and imaginative communication during sex. Women may need to learn how to respond in a fashion that builds their husbands' self-confidence. Both may need to learn patience in helping the other person find maximum enjoyment in the experience.

But can you think of more enjoyable learning than this?

I will share this act only with you.

I recently read an excerpt from Dolly Parton's biography that discusses her "special" marriage arrangement. To paraphrase, "He doesn't ask me about my sex life, and I don't ask him about his. And that suits us both just fine."

Without waiting two or three years to see what happens, I can guess at the last chapter on this arrangement. It will read something like this: "Our marriage ended up being just another tragic western love song. He became jealous of the men I was seeing. I felt increasingly distant and detached from him. So one day our love left town for Abilene. Our relationship ended up as dead as a frozen cow in the spring thaw." A marriage that isn't exclusive isn't really a marriage. Marriage that includes different lovers, occasional affairs, and a "don't ask, don't tell" arrangement is headed for demise.

To establish a healthy sex life requires an enormous amount of trust between two people. That trust includes a commitment to utter faithfulness. Some researchers have suggested that women can only experience climax to the extent they have complete trust in their husbands. Trust is not simply a luxury or option in experiencing true sexual fulfillment; it's mandatory.

We'll discuss later the important safeguards we must put in place to protect our marriages from infidelity, but for now let me suggest some steps we can take to build trust with our spouses.

Maintain the privacy of your sexual relationship.

Don't discuss the intimate details of your sex life with relatives, friends, or co-workers. Of course, if you're having problems and need professional advice, never hesitate to seek out a counselor or pastor. But no one else needs to know how often you make love or what's said and done behind closed doors. That's your business. An important element of your bond is the secrets known only to the two of you.

Contact each other frequently when you're apart.

In a time when people often travel or work long hours, it's important to stay in close contact with each other. It helps prevent temptation and at the same time promotes intimacy. Simple phone calls in the morning and evening when on the road, or perhaps some conversations during breaks at work, help cement trust. We're not keeping tabs on each other; we're staying connected. It's a lot harder to be enticed by someone at work when we've just hung up the phone after a pleasant conversation with our husband or wife.

Compliment each other the morning after.

I can't stress enough how important it is to affirm each other as lovers—not just before you both drift off to sleep but the next morning too. In fact, in discreet ways we should be consistently complimenting our spouse's body and lovemaking skills and the enjoyment we experience from being with him or her.

Compliments the morning after build up self-esteem and trust. They also place our sexual relationship in the broader context of our everyday life together. If good sex begins in the kitchen, as one book title suggests, it's not a bad idea to have it end there the next day—with a discreet smile and "thank you."

Let me urge you never, never to make fun of the other person's sexual prowess or body. Those comments cut deeply and will inhibit rather than enhance your love life. Even if your last experience was a bit disappointing, you can still affirm your love for your spouse. I once heard a wise man say, "When sex is good, it is very good. And even when it's bad, it's still very good." Adopting that attitude will build trust between the two of you.

Talk to each other.

As intimate as the sexual experience can be, it also holds the potential to be quite lonely and anonymous at times. It is far more than a physical act; it is the mysterious process of two becoming one.

That requires sharing our feelings and communicating our thoughts with each other. More than one therapist has suggested the value of looking into one another's eyes and communicating with each other during sexual intimacy. Achieving orgasm is not the primary goal; expressing love and intimacy is. Climax should be a by-product, not an end within itself. There is a bonding in the sexual act that transcends explanation, a uniting of souls as well as bodies. In warning against sexual sin Paul made a profound observation about the mystery of sex: "Do you not know that he who unites himself with a prostitute is one with her in body? For it is said, 'The two will become one flesh'" (1 Corinthians 6:16). It is through our eyes that an element of that "oneness" is experienced.

Husbands, learn to share verbally with your wives how much they mean to you. Tell them how much you love them. Assure them you treasure and cherish them. Tell them how attractive and beautiful you find them. Those compliments and assurances will bring a dimension of fulfillment and intimacy to the sexual experience for your wives that defies description. Conversation and affection are basic needs of a wife; they must be a vital part of your "love giving" technique.

Wives, tell your husbands you love and admire them. Tell them how thrilled you are to be sharing this experience with them. Compliment them on their strength and body. Helping your husbands feel respected and admired brings a dimension of fulfillment and intimacy to their sexual experience. Response from you to your husband's loving is an essential element of male sexual fulfillment.

It really goes back to the basic advice Paul gave husbands and wives in Ephesians: "However, each one of you also must love his wife as he loves himself, and the wife must respect her husband" (5:33). That simple formula can transform a dull or disappointing sexual relationship into a high voltage and fulfilling love life.

CONCLUSION

While a wonderful experience, our own honeymoon in Paris had one low moment.

I had promised Cheryl a dinner for two at a quaint, romantic restaurant. You know, the kind Ernest Hemingway would describe in a novel. And I had found the perfect place.

We had just finished our delicious meal when I felt something touch my knee. "What a woman I married," I thought to myself, smiling. It all was so right—the setting, the tablecloths, the atmosphere.

Once again I felt something touch my knee, but I noticed Cheryl's hands were resting on the table. Just then a large snout appeared from underneath the table. Cheryl gasped. I froze.

A humongous German Shepherd stuck his head up between the two of us and began sniffing at our plates. Neither of us dared to move. One wrong gesture and White Fang might decide we were the appetizer.

"Excuse me," I said slowly in English. No one in the restaurant paid any attention. This was, after all, France. And we were, after all, Americans. As the dog continued to sniff and select his entrée for the night, we looked at each other in horror.

A man at a table across from us looked up from reading his newspaper and laughed, then went back to his paper.

It was obvious no one in the place minded that Scooby-Do had joined us for supper. But we did. We slowly and cautiously pulled ourselves away from the table and headed for the counter. We paid the bill and left the little cafe, checking behind us several times to make sure the carnivorous canine wasn't on our scent.

No, not every honeymoon or beginning to a marriage rates a perfect ten. But it is those early commitments, attitudes, and values we adopt as a couple which will set the direction for the rest of our lives. Learn to give love, not make love. Let your body now belong to your spouse, as well as to you. Make the effort to learn what pleases your spouse. Give an inviolable promise to share this act of intimacy only with your husband or wife. Then learn how to talk to each other, both in bed and out of bed.

These critical steps can go a long way toward overcoming the problems and mistakes we'll make as we learn to be partners. And one more thing. Check your room number before you go out for ice.

Chapter Three

GOOD SEX
BEGINS IN THE BIBLE

A pastor was once introduced to some guests at a dinner party. "You're a minister?" a woman said. "I'm so sorry to hear that. Both my husband and I think sex is soooo wonderful."

There's a good deal of distorted thinking and outright misconceptions in our culture about the relationship between God and sex. The conventional wisdom seems to be that the more devoted you are to your faith, the more you must hate (or fear) sex.

Let's consider that prevalent stereotype that spiritually committed men and women have horrible sex lives because of their beliefs, that the spiritual and the sensual are as opposite as good and evil. This is one of the most important issues we will ever address as married couples. The correct perspective could allow us to enjoy a lifetime of the best sex possible. The wrong one could result in years of needless frustration, searing emotional pain, and possibly even an unnecessary divorce.

Jenna was seventeen and pregnant when she and Gary married. Jenna had been raised in a Christian family, but her insecurities and need for love drove her into Gary's arms. He seemed to offer just what she needed: security, self-assurance, and a take-charge attitude toward life.

When he suggested they start sleeping together, Jenna at first objected. "It isn't right, Gary," she countered, trying not to hurt his feelings.

"Who says it isn't right?" he scoffed.

"It's a sin."

"A what? Oh, come on, Jenna. What's going to happen? You think some lightning bolt is going to hit us?"

Gary kept up the pressure. Though Jenna professed to be a Christian, it was becoming more apparent that she would have to decide between obeying God and keeping Gary—and Gary was much more real to her.

So one fateful night, a night which in many respects would set the direction for the rest of her life, she made her choice. It wasn't long until they were making love several times a week. She felt guilty, but she enjoyed the security of Gary's arms. On top of that, doing something so forbidden was exciting. Although it bothered her that Gary had little or no time for religion, she thought, "I can change that—once we're married."

When Jenna learned she was pregnant, she was devastated. But Gary offered to marry her, and she said yes. "It's not the way I wanted it to be, but at least the baby will have a father," she consoled herself.

Once the child was born, Gary did allow her to go through the ritual of infant dedication, but for all intents and purposes God had little to do with the way they conducted their lives. Quite predictably their relationship was stormy. Jenna soon discovered that underneath her husband's tough-guy mystique resided an angry, insecure, and unstable man. He had grown up in a divorced home and had no role model to show him what it meant to be a loving husband. Before long he came to resent her weak and clinging personality. Their arguments grew in frequency and intensity.

Jenna increasingly felt trapped. Gary wasn't nurturing her emotionally as he had when they first became sexually active. She felt betrayed. Having already been introduced to the exhilaration and adrenaline of forbidden sex, now twelve years into their marriage she began seeing other men. Her secret liaisons—as thrilling and sexy as her early sexual escapades with Gary—were a sweet revenge.

Jenna went through one affair after another. Meanwhile her love life with Gary dwindled down. That's when he began to suspect something.

Now it was Gary's turn to be devastated. When he learned how long Jenna had been unfaithful to him, he stormed out of the house. From there it was a short and quick road to divorce court.

Still stunned by Jenna's adultery, and facing the prospect of losing his three children and marriage, Gary said something incredible for him: "Our biggest mistake was not making Christ the head of our home."

IDOL CHATTER

If I were to ask you to choose the biggest mistake Gary and Jenna made, what would you say? Was it (a) they never really got to know each other before they got married, (b) they engaged in premarital sex, or (c) they left God out of their relationship?

While all three factors contributed to their divorce, choice (c) did the most damage.

Why? Because the most serious error a couple can make is to decide they can build a marriage and love relationship on the sensual alone. When we make sex or anything else the god of our homes, rather than the true and living God in Christ, we have begun to worship an idol, an idol that will fail and disappoint us.

I recently read about the break-up of two of Hollywood's most attractive stars—Cindy Crawford and Richard Gere. He is considered one of the sexiest men in the entertainment world, and she is a supermodel. If ever sexual attraction could make a marriage work, theirs should have been the one. But oddly enough, despite their incredible wealth, stunning good looks, and sensational popularity and glamour, they didn't find lasting happiness or fulfillment. According to God's Word that outcome was quite predictable.

Listen to the prediction of the psalmist David, "The sorrows of those will increase who run after other gods.... [Therefore] I have set the LORD always before me. Because he is at my right hand, I will not be shaken" (Psalm 16:4, 8).

If we try to establish our marriage relationships on accumulating financial wealth, driving sleek foreign cars, pursuing fast-track careers, raising exceptional children, partying on the weekends till we drop, building a perfect body, or enjoying nonstop sex, all these will ultimately fail us. In fact, as David points out, our sorrows will increase.

Why? Because when we make them the basis of our lives and relationships, they've taken on a role they can't support.

David, who had his share of wealth, prestige, power, and beautiful wives, concluded that only one thing was certain and meaningful in life: "I have set the LORD always before me. Because he is at my right hand, I will not be shaken."

CAN PLEASURE BE PURE?

To many couples the idea that serving God first will enhance their sex life seems incredible, if not sacrilegious. I mean, we're talking God here. Surely he couldn't be involved or interested in what couples do in the bedroom.

Well, judge for yourself. Listen to the Bible's perspective on a married couple's sexual relationship: "Drink water from your own cistern, running water from your own well. Should your springs overflow in the streets, your streams of water in the public squares? Let them be yours alone, never to be shared with strangers. May your fountain be blessed, and may you rejoice in the wife of your youth. A loving doe, a graceful deer—may her breasts satisfy you always, may you ever be captivated by her love. Why be captivated, my son, by an adulteress? Why embrace the bosom of another man's wife?" (Proverbs 5:15–20).

What powerful metaphors and images to describe the sexual act. Let's examine each one to see what the Scriptures are, in fact, teaching about married sex.

"Drink water from your own cistern."

The idea this verse conveys is of quenching an overwhelming thirst with cold, refreshing, running water—an obvious allusion to satisfying within marriage the powerful and God-given sexual needs that exist in men and women.

Why wouldn't God encourage that? After all, he created those drives. Rather than saying, "Shame on you for having sexual desires," our Lord says, "Quench that sexual thirst by turning to your spouse. That person is my gift to you as a continual source of gratification and refreshment."

Proverbs says, "He who finds a wife finds what is good and receives favor from the LORD" (18:22), and "Houses and wealth are inherited from parents, but a prudent wife is from the LORD" (19:14). Who actually gives us our lifelong sexual partners? God himself.

One of the most overlooked passages in the Bible regarding God's view of sexual love is found in the Creation account: "The LORD God said, 'It is not good for the man to be alone. I will make a helper suitable for him.... So the LORD God caused the man to fall into a deep sleep; and while he was sleeping, he took one of the man's ribs and closed up the place with flesh. Then the LORD God made a woman from the rib he had taken out of the man, *and he brought her to the man*" (Genesis 2:18, 21–22, italics mine).

Did you catch that? In the perfect environment of Eden, where there was no hint of sin or rebellion, where the world was as clean and pristine as glacial water, God said that something was missing in Adam's life. What was it? A lifelong companion and soul mate.

So in that perfect world, without pornography, adult video channels, or Madonna coffee table books, God fashioned a woman's body, mind, and heart to appeal to her husband. The Hebrew word for "made" means he literally "built" a woman. Then he introduced the two of them. Can you imagine Adam's delight? Just as he was the perfect man, he met the perfect woman.

His response and desire for her were immediate: *"This is now* bone of my bones and flesh of my flesh; she shall be called 'woman,' for she was taken out of man" (Genesis 2:23, italics mine). Some commentators suggest the English translation doesn't do justice to the excitement and wonder Adam experienced when he saw his wife for the first time. My own loose paraphrase would read, "Yes! This is unbelievable. She's perfect. I've found exactly who I've been looking for. Tell me this isn't a dream."

Not long ago a single friend of ours was introduced to an attractive young woman. Later he was asked what he thought when he first saw her. "Devastating," he replied. Maybe that would be a shorthand translation of the passage.

I remember the first time I met Cheryl. We were students in seminary, and it was registration day. I looked out the bookstore window and saw a group of three women walking down the hallway. One was the most beautiful woman I had ever seen. I was transfixed. I gulped. I got weak.

Many months later, after we were engaged, I asked Cheryl what she remembered from that first encounter. "Actually I don't remember seeing you," she said. Oh, well, we're never told what Eve said when she met Adam either.

If sex is sinful and God doesn't want his people having anything to do with it, how do you explain Genesis? Try as you might, you can't find the Bible condemning marital sexual love and the pleasure it brings. What the Scriptures do condemn is worshiping sex instead of God, and pursuing sexual pleasure outside of marriage.

It's clear God designed our sexual needs to go far beyond procreation. He created within us a desire for sexual intimacy much as we have a thirst for water. Through marriage he provides us with a safe, consistent, and loving source to satisfy our sexual needs.

"Should your springs overflow in the streets…"

Here is a not-so-subtle reference to male semen, which is to be shared exclusively between a husband and wife. It's not intended to "overflow in the…public squares," that is, to be shared randomly or with any stranger. The clear implication is that a husband will be sexually active but that he will limit his activity exclusively to his wife.

What if modern America took seriously the advice of Proverbs? The incidence of sexually transmitted diseases (over fifty-three varieties at last count), and particularly AIDS, would certainly diminish.

The very fact that "springs overflow in the streets" has led us to the viral/bacterial nightmare now facing our civilization. The University of Chicago study documents that a man or woman who has only one sexual partner in a lifetime has a 1 percent chance, or less, of contracting a sexually transmitted disease. A woman with two to four partners over a lifetime has only a 4 percent chance of contracting a sexually transmitted disease. When she is intimate with five to ten partners, her odds triple—up to 13 percent. If she has eleven to twenty partners, the figure is driven up to 23 percent, and with twenty-one or more lovers the odds shoot up to 32 percent. The figures for men are slightly lower but follow a similar pattern of risk. The researchers conclude, "The people who are most likely to be infected share one characteristic: They have sex with many partners."[1]

Did God warn us not to allow our "springs to overflow in the streets" because he didn't want anyone to have too much fun? Or did he foresee the horrendous results, the unspeakable suffering, and the slow, Kafkaesque death that such promiscuity would bring?

One of the most powerful and controversial ads of the last decade was done by the French company Beneton, a manufacturer of clothes and sportswear. It shows a gaunt, hollow-socketed young man lying, with eyes half open, in the arms of his family.

It's a hideous picture of death, a picture taken the moment after the young man died from AIDS. God never intended that to be the result of the gift of sex he gave the human race.

Just as God is a jealous and exclusive God, not willing to share his glory with another (Isaiah 42:8), so as married couples we must jealously and exclusively agree we will not share our sexuality with anyone else.

> *"May your fountain be blessed, and may you rejoice in the wife of your youth."*

Here again, the images and metaphors of sexuality are vivid. The "fountain" could easily be construed to mean the source of semen. God doesn't find the human anatomy disgusting or shameful. Yet many individuals are raised to believe that sex and their bodies are dirty, degrading, and unspiritual.

While we're to be modest and discreet, biblically we are to view our bodies and their amazing complexity as a source of joy and wonder—a blessing from God. The notion that spiritual people should be ashamed of or loathe their own bodies and sexuality, in fact, stems from a pagan philosophy, not the Scriptures.

The ancient Greek philosophers believed the body was evil and a prison from which to be freed. They saw the spirit as the only good and pure part of our human existence. Death, therefore, was actually welcomed because it meant the destruction of the corrupting flesh and body of a person.

How different is our heavenly Father's view. God's Word says, "May your fountain be blessed, and may you rejoice [exult, shout, be joyful] in the wife of your youth."

Some time ago a friend of ours took part in his son's wedding. When the pastor pronounced the couple husband and wife, the groom raised his arm in the air and shouted, "Yes!" The congregation was silent, then laughed, and finally applauded. That new husband was displaying a biblical attitude toward his wife. We are to rejoice and be exuberant over the relationship, including the sexual relationship, we share with our spouses.

"A loving doe, a graceful deer—may her breasts satisfy you always, may you ever be captivated by her love."

If there is any doubt that God intends for us to enjoy the physical, sensual aspects of sex, this ought to settle the question. The word for "satisfy" in Hebrew can be translated "to make drunk."

Without question, the sexual act can be intoxicating. The pleasure, the ecstasy, the power of sexual climax is one of life's most exhilarating experiences. Within the bounds of marriage those emotions are to be enjoyed and indulged.

The word "captivated" can also be translated "ravished" or "to make reel." The word suggests a state of near drunkenness with the delight and pleasure of the experience. If that weren't enough, the Scriptures suggest we enjoy this over and over and over again: "may you ever be captivated by her love."

Proverbs is not the only portion of the Bible to refer to God's blessing on a married couple's sexual relationship. The Song of Solomon, or Song of Songs as it's often called, is devoted almost entirely to the celebration of married, sexual love.

In their book *Pure Pleasure: Making Your Marriage a Great Affair,* the authors, Bill and Pam Farrel and Jim and Sally Conway, offer an extended and insightful interpretation of Song of Songs. They point out the numerous references and images of sexual love contained in the book. For example, they point to Solomon's statement, "Until the day breaks and the shadows flee, I will go to the mountain of myrrh and the hill of incense" (Song of Songs 4:6). They suggest this refers to a night of lovemaking in which the bride is likened unto a sweet-smelling garden.

The wife describes her lover by saying, "My lover is to me a sachet of myrrh resting between my breasts" (1:13). The authors explain, "The picture is that he lies close to her heart. Just as the fragrance of her perfume lingers day and night, his love penetrates her heart with a strengthening aroma."[2]

It's clear that God is in favor of exhilarating passion and satisfying sexual love between a husband and wife. If somehow we've sent the message to the culture or to our children that God considers sex a bad thing, then we've been unbiblical. The fact is, we don't have to choose between loving God and enjoying sex. Within the context of marriage the two can go hand in hand.

According to the University of Chicago researchers again, marriage does provide the best context for experiencing lifelong, ongoing sexual satisfaction. Of all the married Americans surveyed, an incredible 88 percent said they derived "great pleasure" from their sex lives, and 85 percent said they received "great emotional satisfaction" from it.[3]

THREE SUGGESTIONS

But if a close, personal relationship with God is essential to a fulfilling and lasting sexual relationship with our spouses, how do we incorporate it into our lives?

Let me offer three suggestions:

1. Place your faith in Jesus Christ alone for your salvation.

The Scriptures clearly point out that apart from placing our trust in the finished work of Christ on the cross for our salvation, we have no hope of heaven. But his shed blood canceled our guilt.

When we recognize our sin and believe that Jesus bore the full weight and guilt of it on the cross, we can receive the gift of eternal life.

It's simply a matter of grace. We choose by faith to receive God's total and complete forgiveness by trusting in Christ alone for our salvation. The Bible says, "For God so loved the world that he gave his one and only Son, that whoever believes in him shall not perish but have eternal life" (John 3:16).

Why is that important to a couple's sexual relationship? Because we can't experience the fullest extent of oneness with each other until we've been reconciled to God. We can't build a lifelong love affair on a faulty set of spiritual blueprints. "There is a way that seems right to a man, but in the end it leads to death," the proverb warns (Proverbs 14:12).

Remember Jenna and Gary? They believed sexual attraction alone could make their relationship work. They made no room for God in their lives, and their love eventually withered and died like a branch sawed off a tree. They weren't connected to the God who offers continual forgiveness, unconditional love, and a reason for living.

The best sex possible in marriage begins with two hearts connected to one God. That requires both partners to experience the life-changing effects of receiving Jesus Christ as their Savior.

2. Commit your sexual relationship to God.

I once asked a close friend from college how he had enjoyed his honeymoon. Several of us had threatened to follow him and his new bride wherever they went and give them no peace.

"Listen," he smiled, "if you had followed us, all you would have heard when we arrived at the hotel room was one long prayer."

I knew he was sincere. He and his wife were devoted first and foremost to God. From the very first hour of their married life, they got down on their knees and committed their relationship to Christ.

When Cheryl and I married, we chose a specific verse for our wedding invitations: "As for me and my household, we will serve the LORD" (Joshua 24:15). Why? Because our marriage was his gift to us. We wanted him to have ownership of every aspect of our lives together.

I think back to the June day we arrived at the hotel after our wedding reception was over. We checked in at the desk and then carried our bags over to the elevator. Just as we were getting on, a couple still dressed in their tuxedo and wedding gown walked on next to us. It was a happy coincidence. We were all starting our married lives the same day.

We smiled at them, but they didn't smile back. They couldn't. In fact, their eyes didn't even focus. Both were dead drunk. They propped each other up as they leaned against the wall of the elevator. When the door opened, we let them get out first.

I've often wondered what happened to that couple. What was the basis of their marriage? Did they have the foundation to survive the arguments, the mortgage payments, the miscarriages, and all the other difficulties life can throw at you? Did they ever commit their relationship into the loving arms of God for protection and care? Or did they try to survive life's storms on their own strength? Statistics say one of the two couples who got on the elevator that day will divorce.

Even if you started your marriage strictly on your own resources, as I suspect this couple did, it's not too late to commit it to Christ today. He is interested in being Lord and Savior over every aspect of your life, including your marriage and sexual relationship.

Through prayer you can ask that he use your life of sexual intimacy to bless the life of your husband or wife. You can ask that it be used to bring about the oneness he desires between you as a couple. I predict you will eventually experience a dimension of sexual enjoyment and fulfillment unlike anything you have known in your married life.

3. Pray together on a daily basis.

Human beings are not divided into departments like an outlet store. We are not divided into sexual, spiritual, intellectual, emotional, and physical compartments. Each of us is one person with all these elements closely intertwined.

When one part of our life suffers, often the others do as well. When we get sick with a wrenching stomach flu, or we suffer from depression or emotional or chemical imbalances, our sexual drives can suffer considerably. The same thing can happen when we are suffering from spiritual sickness, such as unconfessed sin, guilt, or alienation from God. King David, who was guilty of adultery, lay for seven days on the floor and refused to eat or sleep as he prayed for God to have mercy on their sick child. The passion he once felt for Bathsheba was replaced by guilt and despair over the consequences of their sin.

That's why praying together is so important to the health of a husband and wife's total relationship. It maintains oneness on a spiritual level that we desire in all the other areas of life. Just as talking and communicating create oneness, just as showing affection and engaging in sexual relations create oneness, so do prayer and reading Scripture together.

I once had a repairman inspect our furnace because it hadn't been working well. He took out the filter and showed me its half-inch layer of dust. "Put this in the shower," he said. (Even not being particularly skilled in mechanics, I knew enough not to ask if I should use normal or extra dry shampoo.) I laid it down in the tub and turned on the shower. When I picked the filter up and drained it, I saw huge dust globules lying in the tub.

He inserted the filter back into the furnace and then turned the blower on. Our house suddenly reverberated with the sounds of an April windstorm on the Florida coast as air rushed through the vents at gale force. I wondered if I'd have to board and tape the windows and head inland.

There wasn't much mystery about what had happened. Once we had washed the filter, fresh air could flow freely again. The same thing happens when you bathe your marriage and sexual relationship in prayer. The obstacles and impediments are removed. The fresh wind of God's love and purposes can blow freely through your home again.

CONCLUSION

Loving God and enjoying sex are not at odds with one another. The secular researchers at the University of Chicago recognize this also. Although they are speaking of religious women, the same could just as easily be said of religious males: "The association for women between religious affiliation and orgasms may seem surprising because conservative religious women are so often portrayed as sexually repressed. Perhaps conservative Protestant women firmly believe in the holiness of marriage and of sexuality as an expression of their love for their husbands. In this sense the findings are consistent with the other findings on sexual satisfaction.

"And despite the popular image of the straitlaced conservative Protestants, there is at least circumstantial evidence that the image may be a myth at least as it pertains to sexual intercourse."[4]

Perhaps good sex does begin in the Bible. Why not see for yourself?

Chapter Four

AREN'T MY NEEDS YOUR NEEDS?

Several years ago I was teaching a class for newly married couples. The discussion was discreet and lighthearted, but there was one interchange I've never forgotten.

"Men don't seem to understand," one wife said. "They think that just as long as they've satisfied their sexual needs, we're satisfied too. But when they're all finished, we're just ready to get started."

"Isn't that the sad truth?" piped up another woman, who was normally shy, quiet, and uncomplaining. No one could believe what she had said. Her husband blushed seven shades of red.

The group was quiet for an instant, then it broke loose with laughter. Several individuals laughed so hard they cried. The husband was speechless and undone. It took several minutes before anyone could say anything, and as soon as someone would attempt to change the subject, the laughter would start all over again. It was hopeless. As I glanced around the classroom, I noticed a slight tinge of guilt and embarrassment on more than one husband's face.

GOOD INTENTIONS, WRONG ASSUMPTIONS

"The sad truth." It's a classic phrase that expresses the frustrations, confusion, and dilemmas many couples face when trying to understand the differences between the two of them. Why do we have such a hard time figuring out what our husbands or wives need from us?

Dr. Willard Harley, an outstanding marriage therapist and author, summarizes the problem and suggests solutions in his best-selling book *His Needs, Her Needs: Building an Affair Proof Marriage.* His ideas and research have helped shape many of the ideas in this chapter. I agree with his basic premise that husbands and wives have differing needs and that it's vital we know what they are in order to love and care for our spouses.

"A man can have the best intentions to meet his wife's needs, but if he thinks her needs are similar to his own, he will fail miserably. When they [women] assume men appreciate the same gestures of kindness they like, women, too, fail."[1]

THE TOP FIVE LIST

From counseling thousands of couples through the years, Harley believes the top five needs of men and the top five needs of women are different. Although there are undoubtedly exceptions, he sees their needs as usually falling into these categories:

The Basic Needs of a Wife
1. Affection
2. Conversation
3. Honesty and openness
4. Financial support
5. Family commitment

The Basic Needs of a Husband

1. Sexual fulfillment
2. Recreational companionship
3. An attractive spouse
4. Domestic support
5. Admiration

He concludes, "By learning to understand your spouse as a totally different person than you, you can begin to become an expert in meeting all that person's marital needs, if you would like to."[2]

A woman who looks over the female list might ask the obvious question, "Why isn't sexual fulfillment listed among my needs?"

There's no doubt that women have strong sexual needs. In fact, I would argue that sexual fulfillment is extremely important to women. Yet, what many men fail to understand is that a wife's sexual gratification is related to her experience of affection, conversation, honesty and openness, financial support, and family commitment. They all play a part in her experiencing love from her husband.

On the other hand a male can experience a degree of sexual satisfaction simply from engaging in the act itself. That's why it's possible for some men to experience sexual enjoyment in an impersonal encounter with a prostitute. But in the long run a satisfying sex life for a husband does involve having his other needs—a recreational companion, an attractive spouse, domestic support, and admiration—met as well.

SOME BASIC DIFFERENCES

The University of Chicago study shed further light on the distinctions between men's and women's sexual differences. When over thirty-four hundred respondents were asked, "How often do you think about sex?" there was a wide disparity in responses between genders. Approximately 54 percent of men answered, "Every day, or several times a day," while only 19 percent of women said the same thing. Almost three times as many men as women think about sex on a daily basis.[3]

If the figures are reliable—and the researchers took great care to be certain they were—men would appear to be much more preoccupied with sex than women are. This could be explained by the makeup of male physiology. Dr. Donald Joy suggests that sexual fulfillment is more a physiological (biological-hydraulic) response for men, as compared to an emotional/relational (psychosocial) response for women. This does not diminish the strength or legitimacy of each gender's sexual needs, but it explains some of the differences in how they are experienced.

Differences are also evident in the reasons men and women first had intercourse. The number one reason for females was affection for their partners (48 percent of the women versus 25 percent of the men), suggesting a strong relational component is involved in female sexuality. For men the number one reason was curiosity and a readiness for sex (51 percent of the men versus 24 percent of the women). While 12 percent of men had their first intercourse simply for physical pleasure, only 3 percent of women did.[4]

MAKING LOVE AND WAR

But how do these findings translate into meeting one another's needs more effectively in marriage? Let's look at a typical problem—how men and women view sex when there is conflict.

Let's say Jack and Linda have been married for five years. While they can make ends meet, finances are still tight. One day a bill arrives in the mail that neither was counting on. A simple discussion soon erupts into an argument over whose fault it is they didn't plan for this. Unable to resolve the issue, they sulk off to different corners of the house.

Jack, feeling bad about the conflict, comes up to Linda in the bathroom and puts his arms around her. "Hey, sweetheart. Why don't we just forget about all this budget business and go next door to the bedroom?"

"I'm not ready to, Jack," says Linda, wiping tears from her eyes. "What you said about me wasting money really hurt."

Jack loosens his hug and pulls back. "Come on, we have better things to do than argue."

"I said I'm not ready."

"Why not? I was only trying to apologize and help change your mood. What's wrong? Aren't you interested in sex anymore?"

Linda turns around. "That's not it, Jack. I just can't handle taking the blame for not having any money in the house. I do my best to make our dollars stretch, but when we come up short, you act like it's my fault."

"Come on, honey," he says with a wry grin. "I know how we can solve this problem." He reaches for her again, but she stiffens and refuses to return the affection.

"Not until we get this settled once and for all," she says. "Then we can make love."

"Fine, have it your way," he retorts and storms out of the bathroom. "I was only trying to show you I was sorry."

Now why can't Jack and Linda reconcile? Is he using sex to avoid dealing with conflict? Or is she using sex to manipulate him? Or is there another explanation?

Much of their problem results from their lack of understanding of how the other person views sex and conflict.

Jack isn't necessarily trying to avoid the conflict by suggesting they go to bed. In his mind having sex is a legitimate way of easing tensions between them. He believes a pleasurable experience like intercourse will create a better climate for them to resolve their differences. "I'm only trying to say 'I love you, Linda,'" he thinks.

Linda, on the other hand, feels she can only give herself to Jack if the tension between them is already resolved. That requires working through the money issues. Otherwise she feels she's cheapening herself to go through with an act without her feeling intimate or close. "I can't live a lie, Jack," she thinks.

For them to reconcile they need to appreciate and honor the differences between them.

Let's try the same scenario, assuming they both have gained further understanding about their mate.

"What you said about me wasting money really hurt," says Linda.

Jack loosens his hug and pulls back. "Come on, we have better things to do than argue."

"I agree, but right now I'm not feeling very close to you."

Jack pauses for a moment, then reaches out a hand, "I can see why, Linda. I'm sorry for taking my insecurities out on you. I apologize."

Linda looks up and sees the sadness in her husband's eyes. "Oh, Jack, I know how hard you try. I'm sorry if I don't always express that."

He pulls her toward him and gives her an enveloping hug.

She leans her head into his shoulder. "I hate it when we fight," she whispers.

"So do I," he says tenderly. He puts both hands on her shoulders and looks into her eyes. "I love you, Linda."

"I love you too, sweetheart."

"Maybe we should take a few minutes to sit down and review our budget," suggests Jack.

"I think that's a good idea," she smiles.

For the next hour the two of them reexamine their budget goals, recent income, and possible future expenses. They are forced to make a number of tough decisions, but they emerge from the meeting as partners, not opponents.

Later that night they celebrate their reconciliation.

THE AIR WOMEN BREATHE

A few years ago NASA announced a novel experiment. In a remote region of Arizona a large bubble known as Biosphere II was constructed. For two years scientists and others lived in an entirely self-contained, self-supporting world. Everything needed to sustain life was either stored or grown inside the bubble. The goal was to study how future space explorers could create an environment that would sustain life and health in a hostile world.

As husbands we need to undertake a similar project in order to meet our wives' sexual needs. We need to create a marital "biosphere" of love and nurture that allows our relationship to grow and stay healthy.

As Harley points out, affection and conversation are essential elements of this. We husbands often don't see or feel the need for touching and displaying affection as much as our wives do. But women crave affectionate touching and intimate conversation, not just during sexual intimacy, but outside the bedroom as well.

A less-than-touching moment

I once held a vow renewal ceremony at a weekend camp deep in the north woods in which I invited interested couples to come forward and recite again their marriage vows. The majority of the couples held hands and faced one another as they recited their sacred promises.

But I noticed one older man who refused to touch his wife or look her in the eyes. He just stood there, shoulder to shoulder with her, mumbling the vows to himself. She left in tears as soon as the ceremony was over. He couldn't have hurt her any more deeply if he had wanted to.

Why? More important to her than reciting the words was the need to feel his touch, his affection, and his love. His awkwardness with physical displays of tenderness kept him from meeting a basic need in her life. It likely had done considerable damage to their relationship through the years.

We need to understand that women never grow tired of being held, touched, kissed, or hugged. To our wives it is a sure sign we value and cherish them. Conversely, failing to show affection may be one reason many husbands are rebuffed when they jump into bed at the end of the day and send signals they'd like sex.

Last summer I witnessed for the first time a ride at the Minnesota State Fair called the ejection seat. It is a bungee launch rather than a bungee jump. Two long bungee cords are stretched down and attached to a secured, double-seated bench on the ground. Two brave (and slightly crazy) people allow themselves to be strapped in. On command the fair workers release the cord holding the bench down, and the occupants are hurled in their seat twelve stories straight up into the sky. They actually go from zero to seventy miles per hour in less than a second. (Cheryl and I considered trying the ride but decided instead on the tunnel of love.)

Now bungee launching may be great fun for thrill seekers, but when husbands try going from zero to seventy in the bedroom, it's no amusement. Instead, we need to take time all throughout the day—when we leave in the morning, by phone calls during lunch, when we return at night—to display love and affection to our wives.

Talk to me.

Wives need not only affection but conversation to build presexual intimacy with their spouses. Because husbands are often not as verbally skilled as their wives, learning to converse with them can be difficult. As I pointed out in *For Better, For Worse, For Keeps,* men see communication as a by-product of a shared activity; women see it as the activity itself.[5] So the key is doing things together on a daily basis—such as cleaning the yard or going for a walk—that encourage natural conversation.

Whereas men use communication to share information and exchange ideas, women also use it to connect emotionally and to bond with others. If we husbands are willing to try the same thing—to connect and bond with our wives through conversation—we'll meet one of their basic needs. Conversation will have reduced the sense of distance and detachment that can impair a woman's desire for sexual relations. To the female a lack of communication between a husband and wife can make the idea of physical oneness seem inauthentic.

Meaningful communication involves well-chosen words. Remember the story of Cyrano de Bergerac, the homely, awkward Frenchman with an incredibly large nose? He was in love with a ravishingly beautiful woman yet so ashamed of his features that he didn't dare to confess his feelings in person. Instead he started writing her love letters. But to avoid rejection, he signed another man's name.

Over the months his love letters proved so eloquent, so romantic, so tender that he completely swept the woman off her feet. Sadly, though, she believed it was the other man who had won her. Poor Cyrano was left languishing in the shadows.

When the day finally came that she learned the truth, a remarkable thing occurred. Rather than rejecting the homely Frenchman, she had been so moved by his words that she overlooked his nose and fell smashingly in love with him. She had fallen in love not with his face, but with his soul.

There's a lesson to be learned from homely Cyrano. If we wish to create an atmosphere in which sexual love will flourish, we need to learn to say tender, heartfelt, meaningful, and romantic words to our wives:

"You look so beautiful standing there."

"You mean so much to me. Thank you for sharing my life."

"If I had it to do all over, I'd marry you again."

"Just thinking of you excites me."

The result of thoughtful (and sincere) compliments is a partner who feels close. And when wives feel close, they want to express that closeness.

Avoid being Mr. Fix-It.

But saying complimentary things to our wives is only half of conversation; the other half is listening. Women not only want to be heard, they want to be understood. Unfortunately we men often misinterpret what they are saying to us when they share their feelings. We assume they are asking us to "fix" their problems. Nothing could be further from the truth.

Consider this wife's efforts to be heard and her husband's response. She begins the conversation by sharing with him the low point of her day:

"Dear, the car died in the intersection this afternoon. I just sat there for ten minutes...."

"Did you hold the accelerator down to the floor and count to three like I told you to do?"

"Yes, but it didn't work. Horns were blaring, the baby was crying...."

"I've told you before, don't panic when the car dies. Just do what I say. Hold the accelerator down and count to three. Then turn the engine over. It should start."

"You're not listening."

"What do you mean 'not listening'? Did you try to start the car just the way I told you?"

"It wasn't just the car. Oh, never mind."

"Hey, where are you going? What did I say? I was only trying to help."

Now let's try that same conversation but add listening and empathizing with her feelings about the incident.

"Dear, the car died in the intersection this afternoon. I just sat there for ten minutes...."

"Oh, I'm sorry. I hate that when it happens to me."

"You can say that again. I can't tell you how embarrassing it was. Horns were blaring, the baby was crying...."

"It's frustrating and humiliating."

"Yes. I wanted to just take the baby and walk away from it. I pumped the accelerator as you suggested, but it didn't work."

"Well, I'm just glad you and the baby are safe."

"That was my worst fear, that someone would come along and not see us and hit the car."

"Thank heavens no one did."

"What's causing the problem, dear?"

"I'm not certain. Will you please take it in and have it checked out?

"Sure."

"Did the rest of your day go better?"

"Fortunately yes."

Now I ask you, husbands, what's the difference between the two conversations? Which approach conveys that you were listening? Which creates a "biosphere" where a woman's needs are met?

Harley suggests women have other basic needs that must be met as well, including financial support, their husbands' involvement in the life of the family, and their husbands' willingness to be open and honest.[6] But affection and conversation are two primary elements in meeting a woman's needs. A husband who provides that atmosphere will find it significantly improves their marriage and, as a result, their sexual relationship.

THE IDEAL GIFT FOR YOUR HUSBAND

Every year at Christmas retailers offer help to wives who are searching for the perfect gift for "the man who has everything." I could save such dedicated shoppers a great deal of time and money by sharing the truth about what their husbands need most: sexual fulfillment and companionship. If affection and conversation are the elements of the "biosphere" women operate best in, then a fulfilling sex life and companionship are the air men breathe.

A blessing or curse?

It's easy to misunderstand or misinterpret a man's sexual needs. I've heard wives complain that "all my husband wants is sex" or that "he's oversexed." What some wives fail to understand is that the sexual drive in a male is a very natural, strong force, which is one powerful means of domesticating an otherwise independent creature.

To be sure, some men are guilty of using sex as a means of controlling their wives. I object to abusive, degrading, or violent male sexual behavior under any circumstances. If that's present in your marriage, I suggest you seek professional counseling immediately.

But the sexual needs of husbands can serve several positive and redemptive purposes in marriage. To begin with, sexual desire helps steer adult males toward a marriage commitment. The Chicago study said curiosity/readiness for sex and physical pleasure is the reason 73 percent of men had their first intercourse (while only 27 percent of women gave this as a reason). It's my conviction that this curiosity and readiness for sex is an incentive toward marriage. When it's expressed outside of marriage, it becomes harmful and destructive.

I watched a fascinating process occur during and after college—a majority of freewheeling, adventurous, independent males from my college dormitory gave up their highly prized autonomy for marriage. The same guys who loved eating pizza at two in the morning, going fishing for a week in the north woods, and playing football all Saturday suddenly turned that energy toward establishing a home, providing a living, and sharing their lives with a wife.

Obviously a marriage needs to be built on much more than a male's sexual desires, but give credit where credit is due. When male sexual energy is directed toward the institution of marriage, it contributes to the stability of our society and the creation of long-lasting, committed relationships.

The true cost of free love

That's why the so-called "sexual revolution" has been a disaster. Although male promiscuity has been around since time began, this was the first time in our nation's history that it became socially acceptable for a man to meet his sexual needs outside of marriage. The domesticating influence of marriage was thrown aside, and men were encouraged to pursue sexual fulfillment in random, nonmarital relationships. And women seemed eager to participate in the experiment as well.

I'm not sure who thought men and women were going to benefit by the sexual revolution, but it was a tragic miscalculation. The result of free sex without commitment over the last several decades has been a tidal wave of single mothers, fatherless children, poverty-line homes, and millions of abortions. If that's liberation, I'd hate to see what real oppression looks like.

As a pastor I've witnessed from a front-line vantage point the suffering caused by the sexual revolution. I've observed the social, economic, emotional, physical, and spiritual devastation that results from males having free and easy access to sex without the precondition of marital commitment. It's a tragedy. The ultimate gang symbol of our time should be a spray-painted wedding ring with a slash through it.

Whenever people choose to live apart from God's plan for our sexuality the results are painful. Both men and women take advantage of the cultural sanctions to enjoy sex outside of the commitment to marriage, but women are usually left to raise the children by themselves. Although there are other factors in the problems of our society, divorcing sex from marriage must stand near the very top of the list.

A procreative force

Drawing men into committed marital relationships is not the only reason God gives them a strong sexual instinct. It is also to favor procreation. Few ancient or prescientific cultures understood that conception is only possible a few days a month for a woman. What would have happened to the human race if husbands had been given a weak sex drive and sex twice a year had suited them just fine? Would the human race have survived or prospered?

Perhaps, but the sexual needs of husbands and their wives are a positive force in fulfilling the Genesis directive to "be fruitful and multiply."

The bond that frees

The final benefit of a male's need for sexual fulfillment is the bonding that occurs. Something mysterious, intimate, and life-changing occurs in the act of sexual intercourse. A "oneness" of flesh leads to a "oneness" of spirit. When the other necessary elements of a loving marriage are present, frequent and regular sexual intercourse strengthens the bond. It ties yet one more cord around the heart.

Nor does a male's need for sexual fulfillment diminish much with time. The Chicago study reports that 66 percent of men ages fifty to fifty-nine engage in sex a few times a month or more, compared to only 64 percent of men ages eighteen to twenty-four[7]—despite the fact men supposedly reach their sexual peak at age nineteen. As a result of the husband's lifelong need for sexual fulfillment, the positive bond it creates can be reinforced over an entire lifetime.

When the male need for sexual fulfillment is lived out under the plan of God, it is a blessing, not a curse, both to society and to the marriage relationship.

Will you be their buddy?

Besides sexual fulfillment men also need a recreational companion. Often we aren't good at verbalizing what we need, but let me say it on behalf of all of us. Your husband wants you, his spouse, to be his buddy. I don't care if a man is twelve years old or sixty, he still wants a friend to do things with.

Let's say your husband comes in the door and says, "Honey, would you come out and help me with the yard work?" You're thinking, "What did I ever do to deserve such a Don Juan?"

But let me translate what he's really saying.

"Dear, sometimes it's a lonely world for a husband. I'd like you to do something I used to ask my buddies to do when I was single—work on a project with me. So even though it means interrupting what you're doing, just your being beside me and talking to me will help me feel like I've got a friend."

Wives, if you knew your husbands were actually saying that to you, wouldn't it change your minds about going fishing, watching a game on television, or going to the hardware store together? If it's conversation you want, what better thing to do than get in a small boat and go fishing for a day? After all, where's he going to go that you won't? You've got him all to yourself for eight hours.

Don't underestimate your husband's need for a friend. A group of four hundred divorced men who were planning to remarry were asked what they liked most about their new fiancées. The number one answer was, "She's my best friend."[8]

CONCLUSION

We need to remember that men and women have different sexual responses. Because men are wired for quick arousal and satisfaction, a husband can be satisfied before his spouse is even aroused (as the wife complained in the beginning of the chapter).

Men, therefore, need to memorize these three words to understand how to satisfy their wives: patience, affection, and conversation. When it comes to sexual fulfillment, women aren't interested in fast food orders. They're designed to enjoy slow, exquisite, fine gourmet cooking. You can't rush bon vivant food, nor should you rush sexual intimacy. Be patient, show affection, and engage in loving and romantic conversation.

What three words should wives take to heart to meet their husbands' sexual needs? Availability, response, and respect. Be available to your spouse, respond to his loving suggestions and gestures, and communicate your admiration and respect for him.

Some time ago I heard an author on the radio share the story of the near demise of his marriage. He loved golf and spent most of his discretionary time on the greens. As his marriage disintegrated, he became more and more demanding that his wife meet his needs. If she would just let him live the way he wanted, everything would work out just fine, he reasoned.

Eventually he realized they were on the verge of divorce. He went home, put his golf clubs in the closet, and told her he was now interested in meeting her needs. At first she didn't believe him. But over time, as he put her first in his life and learned what she really needed from him, their relationship changed. Their love was renewed. He couldn't wait to get home to her. Their sexual relationship heated up again.

One day his wife met him in the hallway and handed him his golf clubs.

"What are you doing?" he asked.

"I want you to go play golf," she smiled. "It's been three years since you last played. I want you to go and enjoy yourself."[9]

When he decided to meet her needs, it awakened a response in her to meet his. It's a simple strategy, but it transformed their marriage.

It can transform yours as well. Is there a better time than now to start the process?

PART TWO

SUSTAINED PLEASURE: PRESERVING THE SATISFACTION OF MARRIED SEX

Chapter Five

TIME
WILL LET YOU

I 'll never forget the day Cheryl and I found our dream house.

We were new to Chicago and had been renting for less than a year. With four children six years old and younger, it was obvious we needed more space. So we started driving through new construction sites and subdivisions to look for a new home. All over our county developments were popping up like mushrooms in a damp Kentucky cave.

After weeks and weeks of touring models, looking over floor plans, and asking sales representatives if there wasn't one too many zeros on the price tag of their new homes, we at last found the place we had been dreaming of. The subdivision had a lovely, idyllic, rural-sounding name like "Country Meadows." (Actually it was next to a cemetery and a four-lane road, but developers and Realtors are sometimes gifted with vivid imaginations.) When we discovered the home was "almost" in our price range, we were ecstatic. A few weeks later we signed a purchase agreement, adding a fourth bedroom, a fireplace, and improved carpeting on top of the base price.

Soon construction began. We went out almost every day to watch them build our little house by the tollway. Slowly our dream dwelling took on shape, first with poured concrete and blocks, then studs and roofing, and finally walls and appliances. It was beautiful. It was perfect. It was ours.

It was the hottest August in a hundred years when we moved in. Once we were done paying all the extra costs involved in a real estate closing (we were charged for walking in the door, using their chairs to sit in, being alive) we didn't have a penny to spare. But the house was ours.

As I thundered up to our new residence in the rented Ryder moving truck, I looked with pride over our new home and our front yard—which was nothing but black dirt. "That's right," I remembered, "the house doesn't come with a lawn. Oh well, that will have to wait." We had so little money left over after closing that other items (like curtains) had to come first.

As the weeks went by, we discovered more hidden costs in setting up a new household. There were rugs to buy, mailboxes to install, shower curtains to hang, and on and on. Meanwhile, as other neighbors had their lawns professionally seeded or sodded, we waited. And waited.

Winter mercifully arrived, camouflaging our bare front yard with a blanket of white snow. But spring eventually followed, and we still had no funds to put in a lawn. It started to get a little embarrassing. I prayed for an answer to our bald yard.

Heaven must heard my prayers because I received an answer almost immediately. Our yard began to grow weeds. Green weeds. Tall green weeds. The same color as grass. Sensing an opportunity, I rolled out our lawn mower and mowed our weeds on the diagonal so it would give the appearance of professional lawn care. With head held high I roared across the yard back and forth, back and forth. It was exhilarating. I waved at my neighbors next door and said, "Beautiful spring, isn't it?"

Despite the temporary lawn fix, I knew our financial situation was worsening. The day finally came when Cheryl and I sat down and had "the talk." With taxes and assessments about to go up, with utility payments larger than we had expected in our much larger home, and with no money for an authentic lawn, we were stressed out. We considered our options. We discussed Cheryl getting a job but rejected that idea for a variety of reasons—the most obvious being our four children. We discussed my getting a second job. I was already working full-time and commuting close to an hour each day. We hardly had time alone as it was.

Unless we could solve our financial dilemma, we would be forced to seek additional employment and become a "quality time" family (which in some cases means you see each other on Sundays from 1:00 P.M. to 3:00 P.M. when they fall on even days of the month and it's the summer solstice). To put it another way, we were facing the disintegration of our time together as a family and couple.

The cost of keeping our dream home and the pace of life it demanded had become a nightmare. We agonized over the decision. We prayed long and hard about it. We asked the advice of others. In the end we made what I believe, to this day, was the right choice.

Just nine months after moving into our dream home, I pounded a "For Sale by Owner" sign into our front yard (into the weeds to be more precise). We advertised in a tiny circular where you receive a free ad if you send in a recipe. We sold our home in less than a month and purchased a forty-five-year-old home exactly half the size. Not only that, but our smaller home had a lawn. (The Realtor was baffled by my excitement over that feature.)

But we didn't stop there. We also sold our new minivan and bought two previously owned automobiles, whose combined mileage was the distance from the earth to the moon. We cut costs wherever we could. In short, we did a radical downsizing.

But as a result, we didn't have to put our four children in day care. Cheryl didn't have to take a job outside our home. I didn't end up with a pacemaker. The bills started to diminish, our taxes went down, and our lives began to work again. Best of all, we had time once again to be the parents, friends, and lovers we wanted to be.

THE CHIEF CULPRIT

If you were to ask what I think is the biggest obstacle to married sexual happiness and fulfillment in our generation, my answer might surprise you. It isn't a lack of communication, or differing moral values, or poor technique, or even the continual bombardment of sensual images from the media.

It's busyness. That's right, plain old busyness. We're just too occupied to invest the necessary time to build meaningful and fulfilling love lives.

As Lee Stroebel, teaching pastor at Willow Creek Community Church, said, "It's like each year some sinister individual turns the dial up one more notch on the speed of life." In the sixties it was assumed that the workweek would inevitably grow shorter as new technology and automation replaced tasks once performed by human hands. Experts predicted a four-day workweek by the turn of the century. Americans would have more leisure time than ever. In fact, just the opposite is happening. Contrary to predictions, recent studies show the length of the average workweek has actually increased by an hour or two since the sixties.

But at what cost to marriages and families? Let's assume one married couple holds two jobs, raises 2.7 children, works a combined total of eighty-six hours per week, makes payments on two cars and one home, and services an average of four thousand to six thousand dollars in combined personal consumer debt. How much time is left over to sustain a satisfying marriage and sexual relationship? The researchers at the University of Chicago found that 57 percent of married men reported having sex only a few times a month or less in the last year. The figure for married women was even more disheartening—62 percent. That means almost two-thirds of married men and women have infrequent sexual experiences (less often than the garbage truck comes by their home in a month's time).

BATTLE FATIGUE

Without doubt there are numerous reasons for this lack of intimate relations, but I suggest a primary reason is that many couples are simply too tired from too much busyness to enjoy their sexual partners. This general sense of exhaustion is caused by stress, lack of rest, depression, money problems, and the demands of parenthood. *Time* magazine several years ago ran a cover story on the fact that most Americans are running on a sleep deficit. One result of fatigue and low personal energy is diminished sexual interest and frequency.

The unavailability of a spouse is another reason for infrequent sexual contact. If spouses keep somewhat different eating and work schedules, put in overtime, and spend what precious energy they have left on doing housework, driving children to baseball, and watching television, how can they possibly manage having sex with any frequency? On one level, given all our preoc-cupations, it's amazing that married couples manage to engage in sexual relations even a few times a month. The satirist Garrison Keillor wrote, "Our country is not obsessed with sex. To the con-trary. We wear ourselves out working, we are surrounded with noise and distraction and all manner of entertainment.... Considering what the American couple is up against, it's astounding to think that once a week or once a month or maybe just on Memorial Day and Christmas or whenever the coast is clear, they are enjoying this gorgeous moment."[1]

The slide into overcommitment and time deprivation is ever so subtle. If most people knew what was happening to them, I imagine they would change course. But it happens a notch at a time. The end result is two people too busy and too tired to enjoy the love they got married to enjoy.

YOU CAN'T HAVE IT ALL

Perhaps the most needed wisdom for overstressed (and undersat-isfied) couples in our generation is this, "You can't have it all." It's painful to hear; we don't want to accept it, but it's the truth.

Most of us simply can't afford all the homes, toys, vacations, and entertainment we want and still have time for our children, church, extended family, friends, and our spouse. But the possi-bility that my generation might enjoy less material prosperity than our parents did is simply unacceptable to many baby boomers and busters.

Let's face reality. Life is a series of trade-offs. We all must choose between having this and sacrificing that. The reason life gets busier and busier and busier is that we believe we're the exception. We think we can have it all if we will just work a little harder and a little smarter.

I watch the result of that type of thinking on Saturdays and Sundays in our overly busy little community. On Saturdays worn-out moms and dads stand on the sidelines of a soccer field, many still wound tight from the week. Little Sarah on the other team lets a goal get by, and her parent/coach screams, "Didn't you see that coming! Where's my defense? Wake up!" Meanwhile, Sarah, who's supposed to be having a good time, is blinking back tears.

At lunchtime our family will sometimes jump in the car and head over to McDonald's. Standing next to me are strangers, faces tense, trying to make sense of the different menu items being shouted at them by the kids. When young Jason spills ketchup on his designer clothes, the mother loses it. "Now, look at what you've done. Do you know how much that cost? We'll have to go home and change." Meanwhile Jason has forgotten that the reason his mother worked so hard all week was so he could enjoy wearing such fine clothes.

For many stressed-out parents it's on to the next event, and the next. They seem so desperate, yes, desperate to enjoy their day. The result is manic afternoons of people rushing from one activity to another, searching for the joy and relaxation that eluded them all week long and trying to squeeze it in before work starts again Monday morning.

Take one of these couples and put them in bed late Saturday night after a hectic day. Tomorrow promises more of the same. They've spent a ton of money (some on credit), the kids fought with each other in the car all afternoon, and they are both frazzled. Is it any wonder a considerable number of married people surveyed said they had sexual relations only a few times a month?

If we don't decide as a couple that nurturing our marriage and family life is important to us, and then take the radical steps necessary to carve out time together, it isn't going to happen. The years will go by, the kids will grow up, and we'll come to the end of it all and ask why? Why were we pushing so hard?

CHOOSE TO LIVE, CHOOSE TO LOVE

So how does a very busy couple create time to nurture their marriage and keep their life of sexual intimacy alive and healthy? Let me make the following suggestions:

1. Decide that whom you love is more important than what you own.

To put an entire lifetime in perspective, let me recommend you visit the home of elderly friends in the near future. They'll enjoy the visit, and it will give you an idea of how fast life goes by.

Pay particular attention to the pictures on their walls or on top of their piano. Chances are you'll see an old black-and-white photograph of their wedding. Then you may find slightly faded color pictures of their children with hair styles and glasses from decades ago. You might also discover a menagerie of pictures of smiling grandchildren—some missing teeth, others covered with freckles.

They likely own all their furniture, household appliances, and the car in the driveway. But is that what they now value most in the world? I doubt it. It's the faces in those pictures and the relationships they represent that are more precious to them than anything on earth. If they could turn back the clock, would they choose to earn more money or to spend more time with their children who are now grown and gone? We know the answer.

So what does this have to do with enhancing our sexual relationship with our spouse? Our love lives will only improve when we do a serious moral inventory of our life values. If we can't say that loving people, particularly our spouses, is more important than having things, we have distorted and short-sighted values. It's time to change.

Let me warn you, change won't come easily. Every fiber and muscle in our bodies will shout, "No! You can't give all this up! Your possessions make you who you are. What will other people think? You'll be a no one. A no one!" But if we are going to create the one item we all must have in order to enjoy frequent and meaningful sexual relations—time—then we are going to have to make some hard choices.

We may need to change jobs. We may need to be by-passed for some promotions. We may need to sell our homes and buy less expensive ones. We may need to move to an area where the cost of living is lower and settle for fewer perks.

But if you and I really believe whom we love is more important than what we own, few sacrifices will be too much. And the dividends? Time to lie together in bed simply cherishing the moment. Time to walk hand in hand down the street after supper. Time to teach a class at church. Time to read to our kids at night or wrestle with them on the floor or spray them with a garden hose on a hot summer afternoon. Time to ride a plastic toboggan together down a snow-covered hill in the winter.

The choice is one we all must make. Not to decide in favor of those we love is to choose against them. In the Sermon on the Mount, Jesus drew a picture of our present generation when he warned about becoming consumed with a quest for material things. "So do not worry, saying, 'What shall we eat?' or 'What shall we drink?' or 'What shall we wear?' For the pagans *run* after all these things, and your heavenly Father knows that you need them" (Matthew 6:31–32, italics mine).

The secret to spending more time with our spouses, our families, and those we love most is simple. Stop chasing after the wrong things. God knows our needs for living in this world. He's committed to taking care of us. We need to commit ourselves to loving those who need our love the most. If we make that choice, one of the most satisfying rewards will be time to "rejoice in the wife [or husband] of your youth."

2. Choose to give up what you cannot keep to gain what you cannot lose.

Those words are not my own. Rather, they are from the journal of Jim Eliot, a young man who died in Ecuador at the age of twenty-seven, trying to reach a primitive tribe with the love of Christ. Those words have profound meaning for a couple wanting to make time for the things that matter most.

Not far from our home stands the Cuneo mansion. Once owned and operated by one of the wealthiest men in the Chicago area, it's now a museum. In other words, it's empty. You can eat brunch there on Sundays, and you can drive through the grounds at Christmastime to see a beautiful display of lights, and in the summer a local orchestra holds a series of concerts on its lawn. Otherwise the place is deserted except for the small security and maintenance staff.

When Mr. Cuneo was alive, it would have been hard for him to believe that everything he was working for would some-day come down to a Christmas light show, a brunch table with pancakes and crepes, or a performance of the *1812 Overture* on the Fourth of July. But that's what happened. Now the village has announced plans to bulldoze much of the wooded property so they may build low- and high-density housing.

I contrast that with the story I recently read of a quiet, soft-spoken college professor named James "Buck" Hatch. On his eightieth birthday his son wrote a tribute to him, which read in part: "My parents' relationship has been a model of gentleness and respect. Dad didn't wait around to be waited upon. From bathing the children to washing the dishes, he did whatever would be of most help to my mother.... Their commitment to a common ministry cemented their beautiful relationship.... He has naturally gravitated to 'little' people, the ungifted, the unattractive, those often regarded as unlovely, or troublesome, or unuseful. As one deeply wounded person whom he counseled for years wrote, 'You have been Jesus in flesh and bone to me.'"[2] It was this man's love for his wife, their obviously loving and intimate marriage, and their time for others that impacted many lives. That legacy can't be bulldozed or rezoned like an empty mansion; its influence will go on and on and on.

In order for us to build deeply satisfying and enriching relationships, we need time. But it will mean saying no to many things in order for us to say yes to what really matters.

"No, I'm afraid I can't come in this weekend to work. My wife and I are going away to celebrate our ninth anniversary."

"No, I don't think we'll buy a new car this year. Our budget won't allow it. Besides, there's a ministry in the inner city we intend to support."

"No, Susan, we can't drive you across town to attend a birthday party this Saturday morning. It's our day together as a family."

Jesus asked a profound question: "What good will it be for a man if he gains the whole world, yet forfeits his soul?" (Matthew 16:26). How different from the businessman I recently read about. He said his family couldn't live with his demanding schedule at work. His solution? "I decided to get myself another family."

Your marriage is of great value in the eyes of God. Jesus made a remarkable statement in Matthew 19, verse 6: "Therefore what God has joined together, let man not separate." He claims our relationship with our spouses is more than just a legal agreement or a romantic partnership; it is a unique work of God. While marriage won't exist in heaven, the impact of the love and devotion we have shown to one another on earth will. It is worth making whatever sacrifices are necessary to nurture this valuable relationship.

3. Choose to put your spouse and marriage at the top of your priorities, second only to your devotion to Christ.

In college I once wrote to a young woman I was interested in, asking if she'd like to go out with me when she was in town. I soon received a concise but profound reply: "No. I haven't got time. But then again, I guess we all have time for what we want to have time for."

Her answer stung at the time, but the bit of wisdom she offered has stayed with me through the years. We do have time for what we want to have time for. It's not that we don't have the time to be with our spouses; it's that they aren't a high enough priority to us.

Imagine if we gave spending time with our spouses the same priority as eating, playing golf, or watching television? What if we planned our time alone each evening as carefully as arriving at work on time? What if engaging in sexual relations on a regular basis with our husbands or wives was as important as our exercise regimens?

While it's possible for a couple to become too selfish of their time together, I rarely see that happening. What I see much more often is that marriage building is put on the waiting list, like buying aluminum siding for the garage next year.

How can you make developing an intimate and fulfilling relationship with your spouse a top priority?

- Schedule time to be alone together every day, particularly to pray.

- Refuse all interruptions to your private time except emergencies.

- Budget and plan for regular and inexpensive date nights.

- Choose activities (such as walking or biking) that both of you enjoy and can participate in on a daily basis.

- Never accept a new obligation or time responsibility without consulting your spouse.

- Make marriage enrichment conferences or opportunities a yearly part of your calendar.

- Discipline yourselves to turn off the television and go to bed early.

While there are more options than this, the principle is to make choices which create time for the two of you.

4. Choose to be different than those around you.

Keeping a marriage intact and developing a healthy sexual relationship with your spouse is not currently a culturally supported value. In the last thirty years, where divorce and infidelity have become socially approved methods of finding new romance, few voices have spoken in favor of sticking with a marriage.

The authors of *Pure Pleasure* offer a brief, informative history of the decline of sexual standards and values in our society. In 1954 Hugh Hefner began publishing *Playboy.* In 1960 "the pill" was introduced, allowing for the first time sexual promiscuity without fear of pregnancy. In 1963 Betty Friedan published *The Feminine Mystique,* calling women out of their "comfortable concentration camps." In 1969 Woodstock was held, which celebrated drugs, nudity, and sex. A presidential commission suggested the abolishment of all antipornography laws, and Broadway featured the first nude production, *Hair.* In 1971 the book *Our Bodies, Ourselves,* which encouraged lesbianism, masturbation, and abortion, was published. In 1973 the Supreme Court ruled on Roe versus Wade and made abortion on demand the law of the land.[3]

All these events were symptoms, not necessarily the causes, of the changing moral and sexual values in America. The underlying cause was the rejection of the revealed moral truth of Scripture in favor of a philosophy of relativism. Relativism says there are no absolute rights and wrongs, thus we are free to set our own moral agenda.

The disastrous results of abandoning the absolute truths of Scripture are evident. Divorce doubled between 1965 and 1980. Child abuse rates have skyrocketed. AIDS was discovered in 1981 and now threatens to claim the lives of millions worldwide. Fetal research on aborted children is currently allowed by the United States government. Domestic partnership provisions in many states provide spousal benefits to cohabiting men and women, while tax laws penalize married couples.

To choose to find your sexual dream partner in your spouse is an unusual choice today, a countercultural choice. Author Haddon Robinson once remarked, "If you appear on a talk show and tell the audience you've been married for sixty years, they'll cheer. If you say every couple should stay married for a lifetime, they'll start booing." We applaud long-term marriages, but we hiss at the suggestion that it's God's design for every married couple. We want to keep our options open in case the present relationship becomes too confining or dull.

Yet marriage does represent the best chance you or I will have to experience long-term sexual fulfillment. The Chicago researchers admit that when they asked married people how they felt about their sex lives, they expected to hear a great deal of complaining. But the data revealed that 88 percent of married individuals said they experienced "great physical pleasure" from their sexual lives, and 85 percent said they received "great emotional satisfaction."

There was an even more remarkable discovery in the survey. Physical and sexual satisfaction started decreasing when individuals had more than one sexual partner. Only 59 percent of those who had taken other sex partners in addition to their spouses said they were "physically pleased." Only 55 percent said they were "emotionally pleased." And most unsatisfied of all were the unmarried individuals who had at least two sexual partners. Only 54 percent of that group reported physical and emotional satisfaction with their sex lives.[4]

While popular cultural ideas and media images might try to persuade you and me otherwise, the highest level of physical and emotional satisfaction in sex is to be found in marriage. That's why you and I need to be countercultural people and make time for it. We don't need to go and buy sixties love beads, a

Volkswagen van spray-painted with flowers, or denim bell-bottoms to be different. We simply have to choose to give our spouses the gift of our time, our love, and our bodies. That's radical behavior these days.

CONCLUSION

A rock group in the sixties twanged and sang "Time won't let me...no." The truth is—time will let you. You and I have more hours and more control over our lives than we ever imagined.

Time will let us. The question is what will we use it for?

Chapter Six

KEEP THE GREASE PIT DRAINED

L ast spring my daughter walked in the house and said, "Dad, there are bubbles coming from the ground in the backyard."

"There are what?" I asked. I went outside and was directed to a damp spot just behind our back wall. Sure enough, every time we ran water in the kitchen sink or turned on the washer, bubbles would come up as if it were the original set of the Lawrence Welk Show.

While I'm not likely to host "Tool Time" on *Home Improvement*, I know a costly repair job when I see one. Bubbles in the backyard could mean only one thing—money. And lots of it.

I called a neighbor who is a plumbing contractor. "Tom, I've got bubbles in my backyard. And it smells something awful."

"I'll check it out when I come home from work," he offered.

Tom is a great guy. He showed up that same night before supper. Shovel in hand, he walked into our backyard, took one whiff of the bubble geyser, and said, "I bet it's your grease pit."

"My what?"

"Grease pit. They installed these after World War II in houses like yours. If they get plugged up, it can cause real trouble. Stand back; this won't be pretty." Tom dug his shovel into the ground, and we heard a clunk. "Yup," he smiled, "you've got one. This thing captures all the grease from your kitchen or laundry." He dug a short while longer and unearthed a large metal manhole cover, which he pried off with a crowbar.

Underneath was the worst looking, most foul smelling, gray liquid you've ever encountered in your life. "This stuff is even worse than sewer water," he grinned. He didn't need to tell me. Already my sinuses were as clean as scalded dishes.

"What do we do now?" I asked.

"We'll find where the line is blocked and we'll rout it out. But first we have to pump some of this stuff out."

"Where?"

"Oh, a little on your backyard won't hurt anything," he said. Before I knew it, he had dropped a pump the size of a blender into the gray cesspool and started it up. In less than ten seconds, awful looking, murky, mucky, rank, hair-curling liquid was pumping onto my lawn.

"Tom, when does this stuff go away?" I asked.

"Oh, two or three good rainstorms should take care of it," he said calmly.

I looked up. There wasn't a cloud in the sky. Joggers running by our house slowed down, sniffed, then broke into a sprint.

"Uh oh," said Tom. "It isn't looking so hot for the good guys."

"What's wrong?" I asked, visualizing semitrailers pulling into our driveway and unloading several backhoes to dig up our entire yard.

"I think the line has collapsed somewhere near the basement. We'll have to go through the concrete floor," he said.

As a pastor I had been in Chapter 11 several times, but usually in the Book of Matthew. Now I might experience it in a different context.

Tom said there was nothing more he could do at the moment, so we buried the grease pit for the night. That evening as the smell of rotting grease wafted through our open windows, I asked myself what I had done to deserve this.

Considering the possible time and expense involved in fixing the problem, I mentally rehearsed my options. First, I could put the house up for sale and practice saying with a straight face, "Smell? What smell?" Second, I could leave our air conditioner on for the next two years and forget about the backyard. Or third, I could face the stench head on. It could mean tearing up the basement floor, emptying our bank account, and waging war with gray, fetid chemicals most international treaties ban. But sooner or later I might win.

The next morning I made my choice and called my neighbor. "Tom, go ahead and do what you need to do in the basement because we've got to deal with the grease pit. I'll be here Saturday to help you if you need it."

"No," he said bravely, "it would be better if the house were empty when I did this." We both knew the smell could get ugly.

That Saturday I had a speaking engagement which took me away for the day. Late in the day I called Cheryl to ask about the bill. "Well, tell it to me straight. How much did this set us back?"

"You won't believe this," she said. I braced myself, wondering if there was a debtor's prison in our state. "Tom found a simple solution to the problem and was able to repair it in just a few hours."

It was if a presidential pardon had just been granted. The grease pit had been emptied and our lives could go on.

The anger between a husband and wife often resembles that bubbling grease pit in my backyard. Such anger doesn't subside or disappear by ignoring it. If it isn't dealt with, it will contaminate the sexual relationship of a husband and wife because it's virtually impossible for people who are filled with anger toward their spouses to experience genuine sexual intimacy.

Getting rid of toxic anger requires digging up the problem, draining off the ugly fluid of animosity and antagonism, and allowing honesty, love, and forgiveness to repair the damage. Fortunately we aren't in this struggle alone. God himself is willing to work in our lives and relationships to replace hostility and resentment with grace and reconciliation.

NO LAUGHING MATTER

Stand-up comics have gotten huge laughs through the years by making fun of the tensions in their marriages. Rodney Dangerfield is famous for his one-liner, "Take my wife...please." Phyllis Diller only referred to her husband by the nickname Fang. Johnny Carson, in a not so subtle reference to one of his four divorces, said, "My cat's lawyer contacted me today. She's demanding two million dollars worth of Tender Vittles in alimony."

Anger in marriage is nothing new. It has ruined the love life of men and women for centuries. One striking example in the Old Testament is David and Michal's marriage. Michal was the daughter of King Saul. David was the psalmist, warrior, poet, and eventual king of Israel. Michal's marriage to David started out as a promising relationship but then deteriorated into a tumultuous and rage-filled affair.

In modern terms Michal had grown up in an unstable, dysfunctional home. Her father, King Saul, suffered bouts of emotional and mental illness that periodically sent him into an insane rage. The target of his anger was usually a young shepherd boy, David, who had been brought into the palace to play his harp for Saul. His music would often soothe the king's troubled and diseased mind. Yet Saul was unpredictable. On one occasion he rewarded David for his calming music by trying to pin his head to the wall with a spear. The boy literally had to flee for his life.

Through an incredible series of events Saul eventually gave Michal to David in marriage. But when it became clear that David would succeed him as king of Israel, Saul's jealousy drove him to seek David's life. From that point on, the relationships became even more confused. Because Michal at first loved David, she protected him from her father. When she learned of her father's plot to kill her husband, she helped David escape the palace through a window (1 Samuel 19:11–12). Saul, upon learning that his daughter had betrayed him, exacted his revenge by driving David into hiding and giving Michal to another man in marriage (though David and she had never divorced).

Sound like a network soap opera? It was ancient Israel's version of *Melrose Palace*.

PURE SCORN

Whether or not Michal consented to marrying another man while still wed to David, we are not told. But this much is certain—their marriage was never the same again. A civil war erupted in Israel between Saul's followers and David's men, which finally ended with Saul dead and David triumphant. One of David's first demands as the new monarch was the return of Michal. "Do not come into my presence unless you bring Michal daughter of Saul when you come to see me," he warned his servants. The Bible tells us that messengers "had her taken away from her husband.... Her husband, however, went with her, weeping behind her all the way" (2 Samuel 3:13–16). In David's absence a bond had apparently developed between Michal and her new lover, as testified by his trail of tears.

The next time we see David and Michal together, their relationship has disappeared into a grease pit filled with malice and venom. The Bible tells us of a confrontation that happened the day David led a joyous procession of priests into Jerusalem.

As the ark of the LORD was entering the City of David, Michal daughter of Saul watched from a window. And when she saw King David leaping and dancing before the LORD, *she despised him in her heart....*

When David returned home to bless his household, Michal daughter of Saul came out to meet him and said, "How the king of Israel has distinguished himself today, disrobing in the sight of the slave girls of his servants as any vulgar fellow would!"

David said to Michal, "It was before the LORD, who chose me rather than your father or anyone from his house when he appointed me ruler over the LORD's people Israel—I will celebrate before the LORD. I will become even more undignified than this, and I will be humiliated in my own eyes. But by these slave girls you spoke of, I will be held in honor" (2 Samuel 6:16, 20–22, italics mine).

Following this sharp exchange the Scriptures add a sad, tell-tale comment on the remaining days of their marriage: "And Michal daughter of Saul had no children to the day of her death"(6:23). Perhaps her childlessness was the result of natural causes, or perhaps it was an act of God. Because of Saul's disobedience, the Lord had pledged that none of his descendants would ever again rule the nation of Israel. Or perhaps the estrangement and mutual anger between David and Michal led them to give up sexual intimacy with one another.

BITTER ROOTS

What are the origins of anger and bitterness in marriage? A quick glance at David and Michal's relationship reveals several factors often present in tense marriages today:

A troubled family of origin

Show me an angry person, and I can likely introduce you to their angry parent(s). Anger is one of those tragic legacies that gets passed on through the emotional DNA of a family. It's a painful gift that keeps on giving.

Cynthia was a twenty-five-year-old wife who lived near Seattle. She and her husband separated because of the financial pressures on their marriage when he lost his job in the aerospace industry in the late seventies. Finally they decided to see a professional counselor to sort out their problems and possibly salvage their marriage.

That's when Cynthia revealed a tragic episode of her life story. Her mother had died when she was a little girl. Her father had raised her, but to hide the fact from potential girlfriends that he had been married, he instructed Cynthia, "Tell them you're my niece and that my sister died."

Is it any wonder that Cynthia struggled with anger in her marriage? The poor woman had lost her mother at a young age. Then to add salt to her wound, she had to pretend her father wasn't really her father.

A troubled family of origin does not automatically create problems in a couple's sex life. But it does often imprint unhealthy patterns of dealing with conflict that one or both spouses must consciously work to break.

For years Michal, the daughter of Saul, had watched her father's anger explode with volcanic force. Just as Mount St. Helens blew nearly a square mile of dirt into the atmosphere the Sunday morning it erupted, so the royal palace would quake every time Saul went into a fit of rage. When the Bible says Michal "despised" David, it may indicate she had learned some of her father's hot-tempered ways.

One pattern I've observed in adult children from dysfunctional homes is that they are often angry at the wrong person. They turn their rage on their spouse, when in fact the spouse has done little or nothing to merit their anger. The hurt or shame that triggers the wrath often can be traced back to their childhood. *Love Is a Choice* is an excellent book that helps explain this phenomenon of showing hostility toward our mates when in reality we are angry with someone else (perhaps our parents or other significant adults from our past).[1]

Brian was a young man with a ferocious temper who would explode at the slightest provocation. As a young man he hung Russian flags in his window. He eventually developed a fascination with pornography as well. Where did his anger and self-destructive behavior come from? His mother was an alcoholic.

His parents argued a great deal. As a result Brian's home was stormy and unstable.

Brian grew up angry at them but couldn't say so. So he directed his anger elsewhere. As a young man he started sleeping with girls at almost every opportunity. He didn't understand it at the time, but his interest in sex wasn't about sex; it was about power and revenge. His sexual conquests were an outlet for his anger against women, particularly his mother.

Naturally his unresolved animosity destroyed his first marriage. And his second. And his third. He couldn't maintain a healthy relationship because he wasn't a healthy person. Yet he never connected his anger at his parents with the self-destructive behavior he was living out.

If you struggle with anger, don't allow it to destroy your sex life. Instead, deal with the issues from the past that you bring to the marriage. Don't pretend painful memories are "history." Recognize that the grease pit is bubbling and you need to take steps to drain it.

A betrayal and violation of trust

In David and Michal's case her adultery had severely damaged the infrastructure of trust in their marriage. We get the impression that if David hadn't forcibly removed her from her new husband, she never would have come home. Her unfaithfulness sent a 9.0 Richter scale shock wave through their marriage and left their life of trust and intimacy in rubble.

But rather than admit her guilt and seek his forgiveness, she instead turned on David. "So you now run naked in the streets, you dirty old man. What are you trying to do? See if you can still get young slave women to notice you?"

"Why don't you just shut up?" David shot back. "I'm the king now, not your loser father."

But having an affair is not the only way we can betray our spouses. When husbands or wives choose their families of origin over their spouses, the wedding promise "to forsake all others" has been effectively broken. The only premarital advice God ever specifically offered couples is found in Genesis 2:24: "For this reason a man will leave his father and mother and be united to his wife, and they will become one flesh." When a husband and wife fail to follow through on the biblical commandment to leave their previous family and be united to their new spouse, it's an act of disobedience. And the marriage will suffer as a result.

I recently read a letter written to Dear Abby by a frustrated wife. She and her husband have lived with his parents since they married...over ten years ago. The worst of it is that the parents control their lives, including their checkbook. At the end of the month the son is expected to turn over his paycheck to his parents, and they in turn give the couple their "allowance." The wife complained she can't make a single financial decision without the approval of his parents. While we should make every effort to live in harmony with our in-laws, this situation is foolish and unbiblical. Is it any surprise that the frustrated spouse is thinking of leaving her husband?

An unhealthy attachment to parents or relatives inevitably results in simmering anger. But the angriest person in the marriage is usually not the spouse who's putting up with improper intrusions by in-laws. It's the son or daughter who as an adult is still enmeshed with his or her family system. Though they may take out their anger on their spouses, their real resentment is towards their parents or siblings. They want to get loose from the unhealthy relationships they have with these people but don't have the courage or the will to do so.

I would speculate Michal was more angry with her father, Saul, than with David. She carried into her adult life the painful legacy of growing up in a chaotic and unstable home. Her father manipulated her life and marriage, first giving her to David, then trying to kill her husband, and finally forcing her to become an adulteress by giving her to another man.

Had Michal ever focused her anger where it belonged, perhaps healing could have taken place in their marriage. As it is, we are never told that David and Michal reconciled. She died childless, a painful disgrace in that ancient culture. Worse yet, she may have died unloved.

A file of unresolved issues

The third root of hostility in marriage is lingering arguments and conflicts that are never resolved. Month after month, year after year, a couple continues to snipe at each other about incidents and arguments from the past. Perhaps Michal never accepted that her father's family had lost the throne. That might have been behind her ridicule of David's dancing in the streets. "That's no way a real king behaves," she taunted him. David hit back hard, "Listen, Michal, who did God choose? Me or your dad? Huh?"

Some of the nastiest fights a couple can have involve old issues and wounds because they have had time to brood. As days turn to weeks, and weeks to months, the negative feelings and energy continue to build inside. It's what conflict consultant Norman Shawchuck calls "injustice collecting"—storing grievances the way gophers stockpile acorns in their mouths to chew later.

Injustice collecting results from failing to deal with conflict in a timely manner. Shawchuck believes during the early stages of a conflict it's fairly easy to defuse the issue if a husband and wife will both talk honestly, but lovingly, about what's bugging them. If they will share observations rather than make accusations, and co-labor to find a solution both can agree on, the problem will soon be over and done with.[2]

But if instead either person tries to defeat the other or to deny the problem, it's only a matter of time until the issue returns. When it does, it will come back with greater intensity, and resolving the conflict will be that much harder. The Middle East "peace" process is a case in point. Even when there are cease-fires, White House ceremonies with handshakes and photo ops, and an occasional treaty signing, all it takes is for someone to say, "Jerusalem belongs to us!" and the fireworks begin all over. Threats and counterthreats are made. Delegations storm out of meetings. Tensions rise throughout the region. Why? Because the political conflict over whom Jerusalem rightfully belongs to has never been resolved among the differing factions.

The same thing happens in marriage. One spouse says, "What about last Christmas at your brother's house when you said...?" Or, "How about your weight problem?" Or, "Remember our wedding night? Boy, was that a disappointment." And sparks begin to fly. So to guard the health of your sex life, don't collect injustices for future use. Instead, deal with issues as they come up, approaching them as problems to be solved, not a person to be conquered.

To further protect your marriage and sex life, practice simple principles of collaboration. According to Shawchuck these steps are (1) to generate valid and useful information about the conflict issue, (2) allow both of you to make free and informed choices, and (3) make a personal commitment to implement the agreement you reach. (People tend to support solutions they have helped create.)[3] Don't be discouraged because disputes and disagreements arise in your marriage. That's only normal. The only conflict-free marriages I know of is where one (or both) of the spouses have died. Even then I've read nasty epitaphs that served as one final zinger to a mate.

If you can't get past certain issues, seek the help of a pastor or Christian marriage counselor. It's no more a sign of weakness to seek outside help to solve a problem in your marriage than it is to call a plumber when your backyard is bubbling. The important thing is deal with the problem before it does permanent damage to your marriage and life of sexual intimacy.

CONCLUSION

James Dobson in his book *Love Must Be Tough* tells the story of a man named Paul who was raised in an alcoholic and abusive home. Paul's mother died after collapsing in the snow in a drunken stupor. As Paul was growing up, his father routinely beat him and his siblings.

By the time Paul was eleven, he shot a carnival worker in a bungled robbery and was tried for murder. At his sentencing the judge asked his father what he should do with the boy. "You can send him to hell for all I care," bellowed the alcoholic father.

Fortunately during his years of confinement Paul met Jesus Christ as his Savior. As an adult he was eventually released from prison and entered into Christian work. Eventually he married, and he and his wife were blessed with a beautiful daughter. One Christmas, when finances were tight, he and his wife got into a terrific argument over money.

Their daughter quietly slipped into another room and came back with a wrapped package. "Here, Daddy," she smiled. "This is my present for you." Her sweet voice caught him momentarily off guard, and his anger subsided.

"What's in this?" he asked.

"It's for you," she giggled.

When he opened it, it was empty. He felt humiliated. As he had watched his father do so many times, Paul flew into a rage. "That's not a nice thing to do, to give someone a present with nothing in it."

His daughter began to blink back tears. "It's not empty," she stammered. "I filled it with kisses for you."

All at once Paul caught a glimpse of how his anger devastated those he loved. He gathered his wife and child next to him, got down on his knees, and prayed. He asked God to forgive him for his outbursts and for his heart to change.[4]

Anger doesn't have to destroy our homes or our relationships. We can drain the grease pit. But to do it, we have to go out in the backyard with our sleeves rolled up. We have to deal with our anger so that issues are settled and love and intimacy can thrive. It may not be an easy or pleasant process, but breathing the fresh air of love and forgiveness will make it all worthwhile.

Chapter   Seven

WHAT YOU DO
WHEN NO ONE IS
WATCHING

Not long ago I was looking through my father's photo album put together by the air force squadron he served with during World War II. There were pictures of smiling, handsome, courageous young men in their late teens and early twenties decked out in uniforms and flight gear. As I turned the pages, I found photos of men working on planes, officers playing Ping-Pong during their idle hours, and crews huddled in early morning darkness being briefed before the day's perilous mission.

But one peculiar picture caught my attention. It showed a purple flag with an eightball emblem right in the middle of it, flying outside the base infirmary. The caption explained that this unique flag was no honor. Instead, it was awarded each month to the squadron with the most new, documented cases of venereal disease—not exactly the citation a fighting unit hoped to receive. The editor had noted, somewhat whimsically, that perhaps too many leaves had been granted for rest and relaxation a few months earlier.

I don't know who was responsible for helping my father's squadron win the notorious purple flag that one month, but I know one man who wasn't—my dad. Alone, frightened, and facing death on almost a daily basis, he still chose to honor the vows he had made to my mother in a base chapel just six weeks before he went overseas. There, amidst the horror and isolation of war, when no one was looking, when perhaps no one else would have noticed an indiscretion on his part, he still chose to be a person of sexual integrity.

On the home front my mother also chose to keep her vows, not knowing if her husband would return from the conflict that had engulfed the world. But if he did, he would find a wife who had been true to her word.

Regardless of how happily married you may be, the day will arrive when temptation and opportunity meet. It may be on a business trip. It may be at a party. It may even be at church. What will you do then? What will your marriage vows of "forsaking all others" mean in that moment? As someone has said, "Direction is destiny." The direction you take at that moment may determine your life's destiny. Your most important weapon in heading off a frontal assault on your emotions is a decisive commitment—an iron-clad decision to obey your marriage vows rather than your impulses.

THE BEST OFFENSE IS A GOOD DEFENSE

"I know it sounds crazy, but I've developed this infatuation for a friend or co-worker. I have no desire to get involved in an affair, but how can I get rid of these strong emotions?"

That dilemma sometimes faces even happily married individuals. Even those who are quite satisfied with their sex lives at home can suddenly find themselves dealing with emotions so powerful they threaten to sweep them and their marriages away.

Dr. Frank Pittman, author of *Private Lies: Infidelity and the Betrayal of Intimacy,* reports that "Thirty percent of the people I surveyed [who committed adultery]—half men and half women—acknowledged that their sex lives at home were perfectly adequate."[1] A fulfilling sex life at home, while presenting a good offense, is not always adequate to protect us from being ambushed by the strong emotions of infatuation and temptation.

We need to be prepared with a specific strategy to deal with these feelings—before the attack comes. It's no use trying to build a bunker in the middle of an enemy barrage. We also need to be prepared for the enemy's propaganda campaign. He will whisper, "But your feelings are so strong. God wouldn't give you such strong feelings if he didn't want you to follow them. You two were meant for each other."

The only way to deal with such propaganda is by disarming it with truth. And what is the truth in this case? To begin with, just because we feel attracted to something doesn't make it right for us to have it. I might really be attracted to food high in saturated fat, cholesterol, sugar, and sodium. But that doesn't make it right for me to stuff my face with these ingredients. If I'm committed to maintaining a healthy heart and body, the right thing for me to do is to say no to the hot dog or the curly fries, even though it might seem at the moment that we were "meant for each other."

In the Book of Matthew we learn that King Herod was intensely attracted to his brother's wife, Herodias. In fact, the two illicit lovers decided to have an open affair. But John the Baptist interrupted their passionate cruise on the Jerusalem Love Boat by confronting them with this sobering truth: "It is not lawful for you to have her" (Matthew 14:3–4).

In the same way what would Jesus say to you if he were to knock on your office door, walk in and catch you daydreaming about an attractive office co-worker? He would lovingly but firmly say to you, "It isn't right for you to have her (or him). You have promised before me to be faithful to your spouse for as long as you both shall live. Right now your spouse is living her (or his) life believing you will keep your word. Don't let a foolish fantasy life break apart what I've joined together."

I have to agree with William Frey, who wrote of Christians, "We like sex. We celebrate sex. We thank God for sex. But—and here we differ radically with society—we do not see sex as a right or as an end in itself, but as part of discipleship. When we say no to promiscuity or other substitutes for marriage, we do so in defense of good sex. It is not from prudery that the Bible advocates lifelong, faithful, heterosexual marriage, but out of a conviction that the freedom and loving abandon that are necessary for sexual ecstasy come only from a committed marital relationship."[2]

GLAMORIZING ADULTERY

Novelist Mark Twain was highly critical of God giving to the human race the sexual instinct yet limiting it to one partner. He felt it was both cruel and unjust.[3] Some argue that sexual faithfulness in marriage is virtually impossible. A cover story in *Time* magazine in 1994 argued that adultery may even be part of our genetic makeup. Obviously there isn't much support for maintaining purity in our marriage relationships today. All around us we are bombarded with the message, "The best sex is with someone new and exciting, not your tired and boring spouse."

Much has been said about the romance of the best-selling book *The Bridges of Madison County.* I have even had Christians tell me what a beautiful and powerful love story it is. Hollywood, sensing a potential blockbuster, made it into a movie starring Meryl Streep and Clint Eastwood. What's the story line of this best-selling romance novel written by a university professor? An aging photographer comes through a rural Iowa county and meets a beautiful but painfully bored and sexually unfulfilled housewife. To make a long story short, they have a torrid love affair and engage in sex so intense and satisfying it defies description. At the end of the novel the woman must make a painful choice between leaving with the photographer or staying behind with her unsuspecting husband. She chooses to stay in Madison County, and the two lovers endure the tortuous experience of saying good-bye.

Several people who have read the novel confess they wept aloud as the woman made her choice. But when we set aside the romantic aura of this emotionally charged love story, what do we have? A novel about a drifter who comes through town, seduces a woman for his own sexual gratification, and violates the home of an unsuspecting husband (whose worst crime is that he lacks passion and imagination).

I didn't read the entire book, but what little I read left me wanting to weep as well, not because of its beauty or pathos, but because it glorifies one of life's most destructive and unloving acts—adultery. It sentimentalizes the destruction of the most sacred promises a man and woman can make to each other. It exalts the false notion that enjoying good sex is one of the highest goals in life. This is not a love story; this is a story about selfish indulgence and broken promises.

One of the ironies of life is that we cannot enjoy any gift God gives us unless we have the ability to say no to it. If I can't say no to food, I'll eventually be controlled by it. If I can't say no to money, it will end up running my life. And if I can't say no to the sexual drive, it will eventually destroy every other aspect of my life.

Think of the damage that allegations of improper sexual behavior have caused celebrities and politicians in our time: Prince Charles, Princess Diana, Michael Jackson, Woody Allen, Gary Hart, Robert Packwood, and a host of others. Each of these individuals excelled in some area of life, but their sexual behavior ended up overshadowing everything else.

Saying no to sex isn't the same thing as denying we are sexual persons. It is the equivalent of deciding that if you are going to light a fire, it will only be in the fireplace. If it's contained to its proper place at the proper time, it provides heat, light, and beauty. But if we insist on having the freedom to start a fire in our living room, or the kitchen, or any other place we choose, we will destroy the house.

A BLUE LIGHT SPECIAL?

When I address audiences on the importance of maintaining sexual integrity in marriage, I ask them, "Do you see yourself as a 'blue light special' or a Marshall Fields display?"

For years K-Mart stores were famous for in-store sales they called "blue light specials." A voice would announce over the intercom, "Attention, K-Mart shoppers. We are having a 'blue light special' at the deli counter. For the next fifteen minutes you can buy three ham sandwiches, a side of potato salad, and have your 35-mm color film developed for just three dollars. Remember, this is for the next fifteen minutes only. So hurry over and take advantage of our 'blue light special' while it lasts. And thank you for shopping K-Mart."

Immediately a rotating, blue police light on the end of a silver pole would start flashing, and dozens of customers would stampede to the deli counter. Unfortunately over time "blue light specials" became a euphemism for less-than-high-quality items sold at low prices.

Contrast the "blue light special" approach to that of Marshall Fields, an upscale department store chain. There are no sales pitches coming over the intercom, no flashing lights on the end of poles, no hurry-up decisions that have to be made before the offer ends. Instead, clothes are displayed on elegant mannequins. Silk ties are featured in lighted display counters. Personal clerks discuss your wardrobe needs and suggest selections that would work well together.

Which product do shoppers value more highly—a "blue light special" or a Marshall Fields' item? When it comes to our own sexuality integrity, we also have a choice to make. Are we going to sell ourselves for a quick, cheap, meaningless experience—a sexual "blue light special"? Or are we going to place a Marshall Fields price tag on the quality of our character and maintain the value of our marriages?

As married people we will have opportunities to surrender our honor and character for an immediate sexual experience. But as we say no in order to guard our sexual integrity, we are able to say yes to the good things God has in store for us.

RADICAL THERAPY FOR AN EMOTIONAL VIRUS

Infatuation for a person other than our spouse is dangerous, very dangerous. So what practical steps can we take to control powerful emotions that could threaten our marriage and sexual integrity?

Though some of these suggestions may seem draconian, trust me, they are in our ultimate best interests.

1. Break off contact with the person you are attracted to, or have as little to do with that person as possible.

That's right. Don't call the other person, don't write him or her, and don't spend time together. Some temptations are so strong that the only way to defeat them is to run from them. The simple truth is we can't have an affair with someone we never see or talk to. If we stay physically separated, it's virtually impossible to become sexually involved.

Jesus called for us to take radical steps to avoid sin, including sexual sin and potentially adulterous relationships. "If your right eye causes you to sin, gouge it out and throw it away. It is better for you to lose one part of your body than for your whole body to be thrown into hell" (Matthew 5:29). I can hear someone say, "Whoa. Hold on a moment. Is Jesus recommending self-mutilation?" Of course not. He's advising us to take decisive and nonretractable steps to deal with a deadly situation. Breaking off contact with someone we're highly attracted to is one such radical step. While it may be uncomfortable, awkward, and even embarrassing, it could save us from a moral tragedy.

"But what if it's a friend at church?" someone may ask. "Or what if it's someone I work with? I just can't quit coming to church or resign from my job."

Depending on the intensity of the infatuation, we may need to take just such radical steps to avert a sexual catastrophe. I know of several pastors who would give anything to go back in time. With all their hearts they wish they had left their churches and preserved their reputations, marriages, and ministries.

Instead, believing they could handle the temptations, they stayed on and were proved wrong. As a result they lost everything.

Leaving is not necessary in 100 percent of the situations. Sometimes the solution can be requesting a transfer, resigning from a committee, or intentionally never spending time with the other person. But when you need to take radical steps to preserve your sexual integrity, take them. No one else may understand your actions, some may question your rationality, but that doesn't matter. If you know in your heart before God that your resolve to stay faithful is weakening, risk being misunderstood—and leave. Don't tell anyone besides your spouse why. God will honor your desire to flee sexual temptation just as he honored Joseph in Egypt. When Joseph knew he was in danger from Potiphar's wife, he* ran.

2. Bring your fantasies into reality.

Instead of spending time imagining how beautiful it would be if you and your daydream lover could be alone together, why not take the fantasy forward into the future? I'm not encouraging that we imagine having sexual relations with the person we're drawn to. Instead, we should mentally walk through the results should we become sexually involved. Go beyond the romantic daydreams to the cold, harsh light of the consequences of sexual infidelity.

Imagine the look on your spouse's face when you tell him or her you've committed adultery. Visualize the hot tears of grief rolling down your spouse's face. Think what his or her first words would be to you. Guess what the next several days and weeks would be like, living with a person whose face was etched with unbearable sorrow and grief.

But don't stop with your spouse's reaction. Imagine the pain in your children's eyes when you tell them Mom and Dad won't be living together or that you are getting a divorce. Hear them pleading with you as you load the car, "But why? Why are you leaving? Why can't you stay here and live with us?" Visualize them running down the street after your car, crying and frantically calling your name—as actually happened to one father as he left.

Then imagine explaining the situation to your parents, siblings, friends, and co-workers—all the people who love you and trust you in this world.

Finally, imagine the eyes of Jesus as you one day stand before him to give an account of your life and the choices you made, which we all will do one day. What words will you use to try to persuade him that you had no other choice, that the sexual chemistry between the two of you was simply too great to bear?

The Bible is brutally but lovingly honest when it says, "The wages of sin is death" (Romans 6:23). Sexual sin, adultery in particular, exacts an incredibly high price. It brings death and ruin to trust, security, and precious relationships. The writer of Proverbs warns of the terrible cost of unfaithfulness by saying, "For the lips of an adulteress drip honey, and her speech is smoother than oil; but in the end she is bitter as gall, sharp as a double-edged sword. Her feet go down to death; her steps lead straight to the grave.... Keep to a path far from her, do not go near the door of her house, lest you give your best strength to others and your years to one who is cruel, lest strangers feast on your wealth and your toil enrich another man's house. At the end of your life you will groan, when your flesh and body are spent" (Proverbs 5:3–11).

Are a few minutes of forbidden sexual pleasure worth all that pain and sorrow? I know one man who would counter the adversary's inner temptation, "Wouldn't you like to have sex with that woman?" by saying to himself, "And wouldn't you like me to take my orders from hell?" That may be a bit coarse, but just ask those who have made the mistake of adultery. They'll tell you the hell it brought into their lives and the lives of those they loved.

Bringing our fantasy life into the realm of everyday reality is an important step in fighting temptation. It forces us to think through the consequences, not just the appeal, of a foolish enticement. Often the problem with our fantasy life is that it's not rich or vivid enough. It's not that we should imagine in more graphic images what sexual sin is like, but that we stop short of considering the consequences of living out our daydreams. Once we hold them up to the stark light of reality, they lose a great deal of their glimmer and appeal.

A few years ago I wrote a short piece entitled, "What If Beer Ads Lasted Longer than Sixty Seconds?" which deals with the fantasy that men are presented every time they watch football on a Sunday afternoon or Monday evening. If they will just buy this particular brand of beer, they can enjoy sexual relationships that defy description without cost or responsibility:

> The typical beer commercial features young, virile, and noticeably single men in their twenties and thirties. With the simple pop of a lid from a Coors Light, these males are able to command the appearance of their own private harems of young, exotic, and noticeably single nymphs.
>
> No courtship, no commitment, and no responsibility is required to enter this sexual Nirvana. No, for just

the cost of a six-pack, any man can live out his most exquisite fantasy and never have to mow the lawn.

In this sixty-second male paradise, women exist only to satisfy the male thirst for hops and bed hopping. In this best of all worlds, women satisfy libidos without demanding love, they surrender their bodies without exacting promises, and they disappear from the screen without asking for alimony. Miraculously, there is never a morning after.

The commercials are as important for what they don't include as what they do. For example, there are never, I repeat never, wives, children, or heaven forbid, infants featured in the ads. They would clearly spoil the fun, and instantly pop the fantasy.

The message is clear. Pleasure and parenthood don't go hand in hand. The good life is one free of kids, commitment, and crab grass. The daily drudgeries of going to work, changing oil in the car, and painting the house are for the poor fools who haven't discovered a Friday night poker game with Stroh's Firebrewed. So order another cold one, bring on the babes, and forget phone bills, teenagers, and nagging wives.

But how does the Coors Light fantasy square with reality? Let's say the commercial runs longer than its appointed sixty seconds. The young, virile, and macho American male and the barroom babe fall in love. Their overpowering physical attraction, fueled by the high octane of a brewski, can't be denied. Their passion reaches critical mass. He the great stud, and she the mystical nymph, must have one another.

After weeks of ecstasy, they move in together, then eventually marry. Fast-forward the tape a decade or so, and we discover that a tragic—and unforgivable—thing has happened in the land of the High Life.

She, like all of humanity, has started to get older. She no longer looks twenty, because she's now thirty. Worse yet, she's had a baby in the meantime. Its toll on her body is unacceptable. Besides stretch marks, her once Venus-like legs now have traces of varicose veins. She no longer fits in the bikini she wore on the mystical tropical island in her man's Budweiser fantasy.

"Hey, wait a second, this wasn't supposed to happen," thinks the stud. "Life is young chicks, good buddies who like to drink a lot, and blizzards that appear in the desert. It's not colic, garbage day, and wrinkles. I'm outta here," he says. "I deserve better. It would be wrong to deprive them of my rugged good looks and tough guy mystique. Macho-men don't get older, they only get better." But the truth is our Genuine Draft dude is now developing problems of his own. He suffers from a Pabst Blue Ribbon tumor. His belly hangs sadly over the waist, resembling a giant lump of bread dough falling off a counter. His eyes also appear bloodshot. The top of his head glistens in the sun, evidence of a thinning plant life.

Our once invincible Adonis is growing older himself. But graying hair and good times don't go together. He knows better. So to deny the reality of the aging process, our macho friend heads back to the bar. Perhaps, over the next two decades, he repeats this cycle two or three times before he realizes what a fool he's been.

But it's too late. He long ago abandoned his wife to chase a fantasy that could only last sixty seconds. He gave up the love, power, and meaning of a lifetime commitment to live a fantasy no one actually lives.

His kids are grown and gone, and they want nothing to do with him. His "ex" is remarried and moved out of state. All he's left with is a six pack. And as he puts yet another Miller Light to his lips, he realizes just how cold a cold one can be.[4]

It is the reality of God's plan for married sex, not chasing the ridiculous sixty-second fantasy invented by Coors, that offers the best chance to enjoy a thoroughly meaningful and satisfying sex life. So challenge your fantasies for what they are. It is an important step in defeating temptation and finding one of life's richest rewards—contentment.

3. Spend significant time showing love and affection to your own spouse.

I firmly believe that as we act, so we eventually feel. Most of our society tries to convince us of just the opposite. We're told to follow our feelings and act on our impulses—whether it's buying a car, choosing a cologne, or getting sexually involved with another person.

But true love is the result of choices we make, not feelings we achieve. It's showing consideration, tenderness, patience, gentleness, and kindness to our spouses whether or not we feel like doing so that day. As we act out love toward them, a remarkable thing happens: we actually begin to feel love towards them.

An individual at a marriage conference shared some advice his grandfather had given him, "You may not marry the person you love. But you can still love the person you marry." That's wisdom.

Search the Scriptures and you'll discover we are never told to feel love, but we are commanded to act out love. Paul advises, "Husbands, love your wives, just as Christ loved the church and gave himself up for her" (Ephesians 5:25). Paul is not saying, "Husbands, try to arouse feelings of love for your wives. When you finally have the old tingle back, go do something nice for them." No, Paul likens the attitude of love husbands are to have toward their wives to the love Christ has for the church. Christ's love for us led him to the cross. His emotions churned against such a sacrifice in the Garden of Gethsemane. He pleaded for the opportunity to let the "cup" of suffering pass. But it was his will, not his emotions, that carried the day. He came to the end of his time of wrestling by praying a prayer of perfect obedience to the Father, "Nevertheless, not my will, but yours be done."

In like manner, as we choose to speak tenderly to our spouses, affirm their best traits, consciously try to meet their needs, and remain sexually faithful, we find a remarkable thing occurring. The attraction for the other person is seriously interrupted by our renewed feelings of love toward our husband or wife.

What are some simple methods of acting out love? If you find yourself thinking about the other person, pick up the phone and call your spouse. Convey how much you love him or her. Thank your spouse for all he or she means to you. If you have a moment, ask to speak to any of the kids who are home too. Those conversations will quickly turn your compass back toward a straight heading.

When you arrive home, take your spouse in your arms and hold him or her for two minutes. Don't let go. I can't explain it, but something is transacted in the act of holding one another that reignites feelings of closeness and intimacy.

According to Frank Pittman, it's a desire for intimacy, not for sex itself, that draws men and women into illicit relationships. When temptations come upon us, we need to remind ourselves, "This is all about my need for intimacy, not sex. I'm going to find the intimacy I need with my spouse." When all is said and done, we have everything we need in the world to be intimate with the person we're married to. The difficult part is getting ourselves to believe it's true.

'TIS A GIFT TO BE SIMPLE, 'TIS A GIFT TO BE FREE

What is a short list of the benefits and pay-offs of maintaining your sexual integrity throughout your life? Let me suggest just a few.

1. You can relax when others worry.

Just after Magic Johnson announced he was HIV positive, a number of professional athletes scrambled to be tested themselves. A friend of ours who works at a clinic told us of the number of sports figures who lined up in his office to have blood drawn.

For people who maintain their sexual integrity, the latest virus or the newest STD isn't a particular worry. While it's always possible to catch a virus through other means (such as blood transfusions), the risk factors are almost negligible compared to practicing nonmarital sex.

So while others sweat out the lab results, you and your spouse can go play tennis, enjoy a meal at a good restaurant, or plan a weekend away at a hotel as husband and wife.

2. You can live with nothing to hide.

It's hard to enjoy life when you're concealing something from someone else. A credit card statement, a forgotten note left on a dresser, a telephone call at the wrong time—all these things can drive a person crazy who's trying to cover up an affair.

One woman I read about lives with the fear her husband will discover that her daughter was fathered by another man. It's hard to imagine that she is able to enjoy life and cultivate true intimacy with her husband. She's lying to him, and sooner or later he'll probably find out.

But for the monogamous, faithful partner, there's nothing to hide, nothing to fear. My wife can read my mail, listen to my voice mail, or call me any time of the day. She'll find me where I said I'd be, doing what I said I'd do, and vice versa. Under those circumstances it's possible for us to relax and enjoy life.

3. You can practice really good sex.

In the context of a secure and monogamous marriage relationship, we can truly give ourselves to the other person. We don't have to prove ourselves in bed. We know we're accepted and loved just for who we are, so the pressure for performance isn't suffocating us.

Furthermore, we know we'll wake up with the same person each morning. The insecurity of losing our lover isn't there to threaten the intimacy and freedom good sex requires. As we live with one another year after year, we learn what pleases and satisfies the other person. We actually get better at meeting each other's needs, which makes the sexual experience that much better for both partners.

One-night stands, living together arrangements, and deceptive affairs can never allow a couple to experience really good sex, really good lasting sex. It may be thrilling momentarily to go from one partner to another, but it's terribly lonely. Married, monogamous sex offers the best chance for experiencing a lifetime, not just a season, of satisfying sex.

4. You can enjoy a less complicated life.

There's an old American Quaker folk song entitled "Simple Gifts." The melody to the beautiful, simple tune is the basis for Aaron Copeland's majestic "Appalachian Spring." The first stanza of the folk song states, "'Tis a gift to be simple, 'tis a gift to be free."

Practicing sexual integrity rewards us with two gifts: simplicity and freedom. First, our lives aren't cluttered with the emotional, physical, and legal wreckage of sexual relationships that crashed and burned. What about the difficulties the holidays pose for spouses who have destroyed their marriages through infidelity? Kids are shipped liked packages back and forth across the country. Relatives have to choose which side they take. Who will be on the guest list for the graduation party? Who will give the bride away? In short, life gets very, very complicated.

Recently I listened to the soundtrack of a popular musical from the sixties entitled *Camelot*, the story of an idyllic medieval kingdom where the knights of King Arthur's round table pledge themselves to the rule of law and chivalry. The king is married to a beautiful woman named Guenevere. For one, brief, shining moment right is used for might, the kingdom is free from crime and fear, and all is well. Then enters a French knight named Lancelot. He comes to serve the king and queen, but ends up in a passionate, illicit love affair with Guenevere. Such a forbidden liaison, when discovered, dooms the idyllic kingdom to civil war and destruction.

While the musical spends much of the time romanticizing the affair between Lancelot and Guenevere, it does pause for a moment of moral truth and reality. Only moments before their adulterous relationship is exposed they sing to one another, "I loved you once in silence, and misery was all I knew.... Then one day we cast away our secret longings, the rising tide we held inside would hold no more. The silence at last was broken, we flung wide our prison doors...and now there's twice as much grief, twice the strain for us, twice the despair, twice the pain as we had known before."[5]

Give the songwriters this much credit. They know where infatuation, then obsession, and finally adultery lead—to complications, pain, and despair.

But sexual integrity simplifies our lives. We can spend our lives together with the same children, relatives, and friends. We don't have to juggle kids, holidays, or stories about where we were Friday night. Life still has its problems to be sure, but we haven't added unnecessary ones to it by sleeping around.

Freedom is another benefit of sexual purity. We can plan your future because, Lord willing, we know tomorrow includes our spouses. We're free to save money, make investments, raise kids, take trips, and sleep peacefully while our mate is out of town. We're free to face life unencumbered by sexual diseases, angry former spouses, and huge child support payments.

While practicing sexual integrity is no guarantee against divorce, practicing sexual infidelity guarantees sorrow, pain, and conflict in our marriages that may destroy them altogether.

5. You can enjoy a growing relationship with Christ.

Sexual sin effectively dynamites our intimacy with God. It brings the roof into the basement when it comes to praying, listening, and reading God's Word in a meaningful way.

On the other hand, practicing sexual integrity allows us to develop an ever deepening and enriching friendship with God. I have never known Christians living in sexual sin who were happy. Why? On the one hand they couldn't enjoy their illicit sex because they knew it grieved the heart of God. On the other hand they couldn't pursue their relationship with God because they knew that would interfere with their sexual activities.

But a person living in sexual integrity in a marital monogamous relationship is free to grow and develop spiritually. As we saw earlier, it is only the pure in heart who are able to see God. And that purity must extend to our sexual relationships as husbands and wives.

CONCLUSION

The reason God can be trusted with our sexual needs and desires is that he created them and knows what conditions will most fully satisfy them. What are those conditions? One partner, one marriage, till death do us part. It's that simple.

The story is told of the inventor who built the electric generators that powered the early car factories for Henry Ford. Once, when the generators failed and the plant came to a grinding halt, Ford summoned the engineer on an emergency basis. Once the generators were back on line and the factory was reopened, the engineer submitted a bill for $10,000 to Ford. The automaker was outraged.

"Why, all you did was tinker with the generators to get them going again," he thundered.

The engineer quietly took back the bill, scribbled some new numbers on it, and resubmitted it to Ford. "For tinkering, $10. For knowing where to tinker, $9,990."

Ford paid the bill.

Sex is the idea, the creation, the genius of the Lord our God. And because he created it, he knows just how it should work. That's why he has warned us: "Do not commit adultery;" "flee from sexual immorality;" "keep the marriage bed pure." In his infinite wisdom God knows that the only lasting, satisfying, and joyous sex is within marriage. If we tinker with his arrangement, we court disaster. We need to maintain an iron-clad commitment to our vows, say no to our feelings when infatuation would tempt us to stray, and remain utterly faithful to our spouses—even when no one is watching.

Chapter Eight

DIVORCE IS THE PROBLEM, NOT THE SOLUTION

Recently *Time* magazine carried this short but incredible news item:

Prince Charles met the aristocratic but earthy Camilla Shand in 1972, and, in the words of his biographer, "he lost his heart to her at once." Never did he retrieve it. Once recorded telling Camilla he wished to live inside her trousers, the Prince has maintained an on-again, off-again romance with her throughout the twenty-three years she has been Mrs. Andrew Parker Bowles. Now it seems the paramours may be able to embark on a more consistent relationship. Last week Camilla Parker Bowles announced that she is divorcing her husband. Should Charles also divorce and marry her (as many royal watchers anticipate), no law would prevent her becoming Queen.[1]

For the past several years the antics of Great Britain's royal family have provided tabloids and gossip columnists with almost unlimited front-page material. A prince admits he never loved the woman he married. A princess is caught in the embrace of an army captain inside a horse stable. New Age therapists are consulted to help the players battle everything from depression to bulimia to making prank phone calls.

But it is the latest episode, in which two marriages are being destroyed in order perhaps to form a new one, that is the most heartbreaking and tragic in the entire drama. While royal watchers debate the legal implications of Prince Charles and Diana divorcing, few seem interested in the moral implications. Can the prince and his lover dump their spouses and marry each other just because they wish to "live inside each other's trousers"?

RATIONAL RATIONALIZATIONS?

This lamentable drama isn't exclusive to the House of Windsor. Each year in our nation thousands of homes are destroyed by the decision to use divorce to reshuffle lovers and partners into new couples.

Even some Christians are succumbing to the idea that sexual fulfillment is more important than honoring and keeping their vows.

"Sexual fulfillment is a central part of God's plan for marriage. My spouse isn't doing his part [or her part]. So our marriage isn't really a marriage."

"Even if divorce is wrong, God will eventually forgive me. So why don't I just go after the sex I need? I can still have a relationship with God."

"God wants me to be happy. I'm not happy. So I must have married the wrong person."

You might think I'm making up these excuses, but I've watched Christian marriages dissolve using precisely these rationalizations.

While some of these statements are made by people who are simply pursuing their own lusts, others are hurting and desperate individuals. For some it's been years since they've known real sexual satisfaction and intimacy. I had one man phone in to a call-in show who claimed his wife hadn't had sex with him in twenty-five years. Problems with unresolved anger, neglect, impotency or frigidity, pornography, and a host of other problems may have robbed them of years of sexual fulfillment and intimacy. Their lives are filled with so much pain and emptiness that they are desperate to find a way out, any way to end their misery.

CHANGE RELATIONSHIPS, NOT SPOUSES

If sexual frustration and emptiness are part of a marriage, I am in favor of a person changing *relationships*—but not changing *spouses.* Let me say that again. I believe it's time to change relationships, but not partners. Why? Because divorce is not the solution. It creates as many, if not more, problems than it solves.

Imagine that you suffer from chronic pain in your ankle. You arrange to see your doctor, and after a thorough examination he sits down next to you to discuss your options.

"I can see you're in a great deal of pain," he says.

"It's unbelievable. I just want some relief."

"Good news," he smiles. "I can guarantee you'll never feel another day of pain from your ankle."

"Really? You mean it? Oh, doctor, that would be terrific. I'll do anything to get rid of this pain. What is it? Some new drug?"

"No," he says, "I suggest we amputate your leg from the knee down."

Divorce is a similar, mistaken therapy. While it may remove your immediate source of misery or sorrow, the remedy is infinitely more difficult than the malady.

When I was a junior in seminary, four of us upperclassmen rented an apartment near campus. Across the hall lived a divorced woman and her young child. One night after supper she knocked on our door. She stood there with a forlorn look on her face and a mixed drink in her hand. "Do you know what tonight is?" she asked with a noticeable sadness in her voice.

"What?" we asked.

"It's the anniversary of my divorce." Her expression and tone of voice showed this was no evening of celebration. She was a single parent struggling to make ends meet, trying to raise a child alone, and searching for love. Whatever she gained with her divorce was more than offset by the loneliness, disappointments, and daily grind of her struggle to survive.

God wants to spare us those hardships. That's one reason he opposes divorce.

DOING THE WRONG THING
CAN'T TURN OUT RIGHT

The second reason we should change relationships, but not spouses, is that divorce contradicts the clear, expressed will of God for our lives. And we can never experience the Lord's blessing on our lives by openly and willfully disobeying his clear commandments.

In both the Old and New Testaments the principle is repeated: God is opposed to divorce (the exceptions being adultery or desertion by an unbelieving spouse). In Malachi, chapter two, the people of Israel were perplexed as to why they no longer sensed God's blessing upon them. The prophet responds, "You ask, 'Why?' It is because the LORD is acting as the witness between you and the wife of your youth, because you have broken faith with her, though she is your partner, the wife of your marriage covenant.

"Has not the LORD made them one? In flesh and spirit they are his. And why one? Because he was seeking godly offspring. So guard yourself in your spirit, and do not break faith with the wife of your youth.

"'I hate divorce,' says the LORD God of Israel" (2:14–15).

The New Testament is no less yielding on the issue. In Matthew, chapter 19, Jesus was confronted by a group of religious leaders who came to test him. "They asked, 'Is it lawful for a man to divorce his wife for any and every reason?'

"'Haven't you read,' he replied, 'that at the beginning the Creator "made them male and female," and said, "For this reason a man will leave his father and mother and be united to his wife, and the two will become one flesh"? So they are no longer two, but one. Therefore what God has joined together, let man not separate'" (19:3–6).

Suppose I were to take fifty gallons of gray latex paint, build the appropriate scaffolding, and then proceed to spray paint the ceiling of the Sistine Chapel in Rome. Art critics, the Italian government, Vatican officials, art lovers worldwide would be justifiably incensed. Why? I would have destroyed a precious, irreplaceable, invaluable masterpiece. The same thing happens when divorce "separates" the unique work of God in marriage. He has taken two people and made them one flesh, creating a distinct, irreplaceable, invaluable masterpiece of marriage.

Just as in our day, the people who confronted Jesus were more interested in finding loopholes to justify ending the relationship than creative ways to restore love to a marriage. "'Why then,' they asked, 'did Moses command that a man give his wife a certificate of divorce and send her away?'

"Jesus replied, 'Moses permitted you to divorce your wives because your hearts were hard. But it was not this way from the beginning. I tell you that anyone who divorces his wife, except for marital unfaithfulness, and marries another woman commits adultery'"(19:7–9).

Are the Scriptures saying we may have to live with sexual frustration and emptiness for a lifetime because of our wedding vows? In some cases that may be the cost of obedience. I remember reading the story of a Canadian couple who lived in the 1930s. Their marriage was filled with love and affection for one another until one day, without warning, the man's wife began acting out bizarre behavior. She was eventually diagnosed with schizophrenia and confined to a mental health facility.

For thirty years the husband faithfully visited his wife although she never improved. He tried bringing her home for a few visits, but she became frightened and upset, and he was forced to return her to the institution.

From the time she left home until her death, he was never able to enjoy marital intimacy with his wife again. Yet, because of his powerful faith in God and his commitment to his vows, he was given the grace to go on loving and caring for her.

Heaven will reveal what reward this remarkable man will inherit for his faithfulness to his ailing wife. But I am convinced God will appropriately honor this man who kept his vows, even when it hurt to do so.

But in most cases it's not God's plan that a couple go a lifetime without true sexual intimacy and fulfillment in their marriage. Scripture makes it clear that God expects husbands and wives to enjoy sexual intimacy with each other: "Do not deprive each other except by mutual consent and for a time, so that you may devote yourselves to prayer. Then come together again so that Satan will not tempt you because of your lack of self-control" (1 Corinthians 7:5).

The fact that divorce is not an acceptable solution to a frustrating marriage or sex life is implied a few paragraphs later. "To the married I give this command (not I, but the Lord): A wife must not separate from her husband. But if she does, she must remain unmarried or else be reconciled to her husband. And a husband must not divorce his wife" (7:10–11).

Paul clearly teaches that a regular, consistent, committed sexual relationship between a husband and wife is part of God's plan for marriage. But he is equally clear that divorce is not the answer if there are sexual problems.

THE STATISTICS SAY STAY TOGETHER

"Bob, it's all well and good for you to say we should keep our vows. But the truth is I'm tired of being sexually frustrated. It may not be God's plan for me to divorce and find someone else, but it's my choice, okay?"

Let's assume for a moment that you're right. You certainly do have a right to make your own choices. People today do seem to care more about what works than what's right or wrong. So let's start there. Will divorce and remarriage ultimately solve your marital problems and satisfy your sexual needs?

Let's go back to the findings of the University of Chicago researchers. They approached this study with no preconceived notions about what's right or wrong with divorce. After surveying 3,400 randomly chosen Americans, they were surprised by what they discovered.

They considered the popular notion that the "sexiest of the sexy" were the unmarried, the youthful divorced, and those involved in extramarital relationships. But what they found was just the opposite. The group having the most sex was the married people. In fact, the unmarried, the youthful divorced, and those having affairs were actually having the least sex.[2]

Divorced men claim it's much more difficult to find a mate the second time around. The vast majority of women who are similar in age and education are already married. In fact, one man remarked that he felt "invisible" to the rest of society.

The news is even worse for women. Researchers found that divorced women have a difficult time meeting a prospective partner because of the social structures that limit the market of available men.[3] While divorced men may be able to attract a younger woman with their wealth and lack of responsibilities, a divorced woman of the same age finds almost no one available.[4] The best news the researchers could offer divorced women is that older people without a partner think less about sex and can live happy and fulfilling lives without it.[5]

It's not just the Chicago study that suggests divorce can be quite damaging to a person's hopes for happiness and fulfillment. One study found that people's best chance for experiencing contentment in marriage is to stay with the same person their entire lifetime.[6] Another study discovered that a person's reported level of well-being and contentment declines with each divorce and remarriage, rather than increases. This is particularly true for women.[7]

THE IMPACT ON YOUR SEX LIFE

It doesn't take university level research to see the problems and threats divorce poses to sexual satisfaction and fulfillment. Consider the practical, day-to-day impact of the dissolution of a marriage.

First, our mates are no longer available to us on a regular, consistent basis as sexual partners—a reality that is often ignored in the rush toward a divorce. And the statistics argue that finding a replacement for a spouse is a difficult, at times nearly impossible, task.

Second, if we choose to have sex with someone else before the divorce is final, we must live with the stigma and guilt of adultery. (And if we divorce our spouse for unbiblical reasons and remarry, we are still guilty of adultery, according to Matthew 19:9.) Until the divorce decree is granted, we don't have the option of marrying our new sexual partners. If someone is willing to have sex with us, despite the fact we're still married, it should put some question in our minds about their reliability and character as future mates. If they will cheat *with* us now, what will prevent them from cheating *on* us later?

Or, choice number three is to have intermittent and irregular intercourse with our spouses until the divorce is final (and perhaps occasionally afterwards). So while we're legally cutting them out of our lives, we are still bonding with them in bed. That sounds like a formula for considerable emotional confusion and anxiety, certainly not a recipe for sexual fulfillment or contentment.

Should we eventually remarry, statistically the chance of a second marriage ending in divorce is higher than for the first marriage.

Now we must also reckon with the stress factors of blended families, child support payments, a decreased standard of living (especially for women), the emotional wounds inflicted on our children, plus all the pressure of trying to make a second marriage work (often with people who also failed in their previous marriages).

In comparison to these problems, doesn't working out our frustrations and difficulties with our present husbands or wives sound like a simpler option? Divorce can be described in a variety of ways, but the word that describes it best is *complicated.*

So what's the answer? If there are sexual problems in our relationships, we need to deal with them. We need to communicate openly with our spouses. Perhaps we will need to seek counseling. If our spouses won't go, we can go. Unless one spouse acts to change the situation, everything will stay the same.

We need to get at the root problems of the sexual dysfunction. It may go back to an incident of sexual abuse in childhood. It may be related to depression or unresolved guilt or anger. It may be a physical problem that can be treated. It might be the result of a substance abuse. (As many as 40 percent of all alcoholics struggle with impotency.)

But if our present relationships aren't working, breaking our vows will merely add one problem to another. It will become the problem, not the solution.

SUFFER NOT THE LITTLE CHILDREN

Of all the reasons to work out our marital and sexual problems without divorcing, perhaps the most compelling reason is our children. They will carry the impact of the divorce for the rest of their lives. Children who were raised in divorced homes tend to grow up with numerous emotional issues to negotiate, tend to marry earlier, and are more likely to divorce than children whose homes remained intact.

A few summers ago I had the opportunity to speak at a summer camp for fifth and sixth graders. One boy whom I'll call Jake stood out from the others. He wore the same tattered army shirt every day. He scowled when others tried to talk to him. He fought with the other boys. He was one tough kid.

One day Jake and I happened to climb on the floating diving raft at the same time. "How are you?" I asked.

"You know something, your talks in the morning _____" was his only reply. I've gotten some tough critiques of my sermons, but I admit no one had ever described them that way before. I took his critique not as an insult but as a plea for attention, because angry kids are usually hurting kids.

The next few days several of us went out of our way to try to develop a relationship with Jake. Slowly his tough-guy image began to melt. By the end of the week, when an invitation was given for the boys and girls to accept Christ as their personal Savior, Jake raised his hand. As we prayed together that night, Jake poured out his story.

His parents were divorced. His mom worked night and day. His dad paid no attention to him. He felt like he was on his own in the world. "The whole thing stinks," he said.

Do we really want to do that to our children? Don't we owe them something better? While divorce may appear to be an solution to our problems, it's just the beginning of their perplexities and pain.

CONCLUSION

The simplest advice I can give about divorce is this: don't even think about it. Don't let it become the back door to your dream house that you use to run from your problems. Instead, turn and face your issues. Sure they may be difficult. Improvement may come at a painfully slow pace. It may not seem worth all the suffering at times.

But the alternatives are worse.

PART THREE

You Don't Send Me Flowers Anymore: Restoring the Passion

Chapter Nine

HOW TO RECONNECT A DISCONNECTED SEX LIFE

W hen I was a college student, I spent time in Sweden. I was fascinated to learn why so many people—almost a third of the population—left the country and immigrated to America during the nineteenth century. My own ancestors were included in that mass exodus.

One reason for the departure, I was told, was that each generation divided their farmland equally among their children. Each subsequent generation subdivided the land once again among their heirs. Finally the plots of land became so small no one could make a living from them.

That same principle explains why many married couples can't achieve the level of sexual intimacy they desire. One or both are divided and subdivided among numerous sexual partners from the past. Because the sexual act is a bonding process, making two become one, we leave something of ourselves behind with each person with whom we've had sex. Ultimately we can become so diminished we have little of ourselves left to give our husbands or wives.

If we are to create, preserve, and restore sexual intimacy in our marriages, we need to deal with our diminished selves. But how? How can the scattered pieces of who we are, pieces that have been fused to others, be brought back into a whole person again?

Fortunately, God has an answer. But first we must understand why sexual intercourse with numerous, or even just one other person besides our spouses, can leave us diminished and divided.

A THOUSAND LOVERS

One man who experienced the painful reality of a diminished self was Solomon, the ancient king of Israel. According to the Bible he had as many as a thousand sexual partners in his lifetime. That has to be some kind of record.

Listen to his biography: "King Solomon, however, loved many foreign women besides Pharaoh's daughter—Moabites, Ammonites, Edomites, Sidonians and Hittites. They were from nations about which the LORD had told the Israelites, 'You must not intermarry with them, because they will surely turn your hearts after their gods.' Nevertheless, Solomon held fast to them in love. He had seven hundred wives of royal birth and three hundred concubines, and his wives led him astray" (1 Kings 11:1–3).

Try to comprehend that for a moment. Seven hundred wives of royal birth and three hundred additional, available sexual partners. Solomon had a thousand—count that—a thousand lovers. If ever a man on the face of the earth had the ultimate opportunity to live in a continual sexual paradise, it was Solomon. Mathematically speaking, he could have had a different lover every day for nearly three years at a time. But rather than multiplying Solomon's happiness, his lovers divided him, over and over and over again. By the end of his life, he was an unhappy, cynical, spiritually unfocused person.

CHASING AFTER THE WIND

Many biblical scholars believe the book of Ecclesiastes was written by Solomon as his personal memoirs, a collection of the lessons he had learned in his life. To listen to the author's description of pushing pleasure to its limits certainly sounds like Solomon. "I thought in my heart, 'Come now, I will test you with pleasure to find out what is good.'

"...I amassed silver and gold for myself, and the treasure of kings and provinces. I acquired men and women singers, and a harem as well—the delights of the heart of man....

"I denied myself nothing my eyes desired; I refused my heart no pleasure.... Yet when I surveyed all that my hands had done and what I had toiled to achieve, everything was meaningless, a chasing after the wind; nothing was gained under the sun" (Ecclesiastes 2:1, 8–11).

Solomon wasn't the kind of guy to be content with one woman at a time. If he attended a Broadway play and saw a chorus line of dancing women, he married the entire group. He had the honeymoon suite in the Golan Heights Hotel permanently booked in his name. His wedding photo albums could fill a library. In short, he lived out a common fantasy among men— one new sexual experience after another. But when all was done, listen to what he said, "Everything was meaningless, a chasing after the wind."

How could he say that? Why wasn't he the most contented, fulfilled, and satisfied man on planet Earth?

The reason is simple and profound: people who have been involved in one sexual relationship after another lose a sense of their own identity. They don't know who they are any longer. Emptiness and loneliness replace identity and fulfillment. That was the life story of Solomon. Sex became a major reason for his undoing. A brief look at Solomon's autobiography underscores this truth.

When Solomon was a young man, he inherited the throne just before his father David died. The responsibilities of running an entire kingdom shook him. He knew he was in over his head. But he turned to the right person for help. He went before God and prayed, "Now, O LORD my God, you have made your servant king in place of my father David. But I am only a little child and do not know how to carry out my duties.... So give your servant a discerning heart to govern your people and to distinguish between right and wrong" (1 Kings 3:7, 9).

God answered his prayer. "Since you have asked for this and not for long life or wealth for yourself, nor have asked for the death of your enemies but for discernment in administering justice, I will do what you have asked. I will give you a wise and discerning heart, so that there will never have been anyone like you, nor will there ever be." (3:11–12).

Few men have ever received a clearer sense of identity and mission in life than Solomon. And God kept his word. Solomon became the wisest, richest, and most powerful monarch of his day.

Yet decades later, after dividing himself with one woman after another, Solomon's character had changed significantly. He was no longer the innocent, frightened young man pleading with God for help in running the kingdom. "As Solomon grew old, his wives turned his heart after other gods, and his heart was not fully devoted to the LORD his God, as the heart of David his father had been. He followed Ashtoreth the goddess of the Sidonians, and Molech the detestable god of the Ammonites.... On a hill east of Jerusalem, Solomon built a high place for Chemosh the detestable god of Moab, and for Molech the detestable god of the Ammonites" (11:4–5, 7).

You might ask, "So what's the big deal? He set up some statues around town to keep his wives happy. No harm done. And what does that have to do with his sex life?" These were no ordinary statues. The worship of these foreign gods included performing perverse sexual acts out in the open as forms of worship. Furthermore, Molech was worshiped by offering live infants as sacrifices. As a fire burned white hot inside these hollow idols, little children would be placed on glowing metal shelves and allowed to roll down into the flames.

Solomon once knew who he was and whom he belonged to. But he divided his body (and his heart) with so many women that he forgot who he was and what God had done for him. The Scriptures say, "As Solomon grew old, his wives turned his heart after other gods, and his heart was not fully devoted to the LORD his God" (1 Kings 11:4).

Sexual experimentation and intercourse outside of God's plan change us. They move us in directions we never believed we'd go. They diminish our sense of commitment and identity. They allow our hearts to be turned from God to other things. Eventually even the act of sex becomes "meaningless" and "a chasing after the wind."

How can this happen?

THE FROZEN TONGUE PRINCIPLE

Individuals who bring with them a history of sexual activity with multiple partners often struggle with a sense of disconnectedness.

Jim Dethmer, a gifted writer and speaker, explains the process with an analogy: "Some night when the temperature is below freezing, go outside, get your tongue wet, and hold it to a metal pipe. In a few minutes your tongue will freeze to the pipe. Now walk away. Ahh!

"It works the same way with sex. People may say, 'I'll fuse myself to this person and walk away.' You won't walk away without leaving part of yourself on the frozen bedpost.... People who are disconnected are incapable of deep-seated joy. You can still have happiness. But happiness wears off because there is always a morning after. One of the great benefits of sexual purity is being whole, clean, guilt free, shame free."[1]

HONEY, I SHRUNK MY SOUL

As a bachelor in my early twenties I did my own laundry. It was through several painful experiences that I discovered not to wash my bright red T-shirts with my white socks, nor leave permanent press pants crumpled in the dryer for two hours, nor twist the dial to hot water for every load. My learning curve shot straight up as I had to throw away pink socks, wrinkled pants that looked like polyester raisin skins, and cotton shirts reduced to fit a Ken doll. I found out just how easy it was to ruin or shrink something of real value to me.

In like manner I have watched people unintentionally shrink their own souls. The debilitating effect of sexual promiscuity reduced their capacity to trust others, care for themselves, and accept love. It didn't happen overnight. Rather, as the years wore on, they lost more and more a sense of who they were. Eventually they found it difficult to function in several aspects of their lives.

Besides the reduction of their personhood, their quality of

relationships declined. The next sexual partner often seemed a step down from the last person. Their standards started to diminish. Finally some were willing to have a sexual relationship with almost anyone who was interested.

Listen to one woman's story of being diminished in an affair to the point of self-destruction:

> Our lovemaking sessions became less and less frequent. During our final meeting I actually found myself begging Stan for the sex he was no longer interested in....
>
> That was the turning point: Like an alcoholic, I'd bottomed out, finally realizing how weak and pathetic I had become. If I didn't get out of this harmful relationship, and soon, it would destroy me.[2]

Men or women who have had multiple sex partners outside of marriage run the risk of losing their sense of purpose in life. In some cases they anesthetize their pain and emptiness with drugs, alcohol, or overeating. They also seem drawn to other disconnected individuals like themselves. When they get together, the result is not two whole people but two empty people who are left with gaping and unfulfilled needs.

The Apostle Paul warned against dividing ourselves with others: "Do you not know that your bodies are members of Christ himself? Shall I then take the members of Christ and unite them with a prostitute? Never! Do you not know that he who unites himself with a prostitute is one with her in body? For it is said, 'The two will become one flesh.' But he who unites himself with the Lord is one with him in spirit. Flee from sexual immorality. All other sins a man commits are outside his body, but he who sins sexually sins against his own body" (1 Corinthians 6:15–18).

It's simply not possible for us to unite ourselves sexually with one person after another and leave those relationships as an undivided person. We have become "one flesh" with them. That's more than just a physical description of intercourse; it's a word picture of the soul-fusing that occurs as well. As Jim Dethmer points out, you can't freeze your tongue to a metal bar, then tear it off without leaving something of it behind. Imagine freezing your tongue and tearing it away five, ten, or fifty-five times?

THE ROAD TO HEALING

So how do we restore a sense of wholeness and connectedness to our lives if we've divided ourselves among others? Let me offer Dethmer's three suggestions.

1. We need to become reconnected to ourselves.

We are all given an equal amount of sexual integrity at the beginning of our lives. This purity and virtue is priceless. If invested in one lifetime, monogamous, marital relationship, the dividends are enormous. But each time we invest ourselves in a sexual relationship with a new partner who is not our spouse, we take that integrity and virtue and give part of it away.

But there is hope for gaining wholeness again. That hope begins with the realization that dividing ourselves among one or more sexual partners outside of marriage was a big mistake. Turning to God, we need to admit our sins, pray for those previous soul bonds to be broken, and ask him to restore the diminished segments of our person. His healing power and grace will restore us to personal wholeness and sexual integrity.

David, a man who had known sexual sin in his own life, describes the beautiful, healing work of God in a person's life,

"The LORD is my shepherd, I shall not be in want. He makes me lie down in green pastures, he leads me beside quiet waters, *he restores my soul....* Surely goodness and love will follow me all the days of my life, and I will dwell in the house of the LORD forever" (Psalm 23:1–3, 6, italics mine).

After World War II the French government made a concerted effort to try to recover its lost art treasures. Many of these priceless portraits, statues, and other artistic works had been distributed by the Germans to several different cities and locations. The French government's objective was to gather all the priceless art treasures and return to them to their rightful owners—the French people.

In much the same fashion God gathers the pieces of ourselves we've given away to others and returns them to us. Psalm 23 promises, "He restores my soul." That's another way of saying he gives us back the wholeness we've lost. Our Heavenly Father has the divine power to knit back together the fragmented pieces of our soul lost to sin.

How? I can't fully explain the process; it's a mystery. But listen to the promise of 2 Corinthians 5:17: "Therefore, if anyone is in Christ, he is a new creation; the old has gone, the new has come! All this is from God, who reconciled us to himself through Christ."

In miraculous fashion his grace is able to make us a new person, a complete person. We have all of ourselves to give to the one person we should become "one flesh" with—our spouses.

2. We need to be reconnected to others.

Steve had been raised in a divorced home in California. Although he was a computer programmer with a brilliant mind, his troubled past and chaotic family of origin left him an angry, confused adult. He made it his goal to seduce women who had never had sex before in their lives. "I ruined a number of lives," he said with sadness in his voice. "I'm not even sure why I did it."

That's what sexual promiscuity, either before or during marriage, does to our intimacy skills. Rather than increasing our ability to enjoy a meaningful and intimate sexual relationship, it deadens and destroys it. It makes us numb to the sense of connection sex is meant to offer in the context of marriage.

Listen to how sexual promiscuity disconnected one woman from her relationships with her husband and family: "As the months stretched into one year, then two, my family began to feel the effect of my infidelity, although they had no idea what was going on. As I grew more distant, Tim (my husband) immersed himself even further in his work, assuming my lack of interest was just a part of middle-aged marriage. My son was angry because I had become unreliable, often forgetting to bring the car home in time for him to drive to his part-time job. Normally, I would have felt terrible about betraying their trust, but now I just convinced myself that I wasn't really hurting them."[3]

Notice, this woman's sexual behavior made her "more distant" from her family. Her son found her unreliable. She began forgetting commitments and appointments. Her husband and she drifted apart.

Our human emotions simply won't allow us to connect and disconnect with numerous partners without damaging our inner circuitry. The result is that we lose the ability to feel hurt over the way we are hurting others.

One of the ultimate forms of disconnecting from other people is the willingness to abort a child for convenience. Sexual promiscuity can dull our inner souls until the possibility of taking a life is no longer unthinkable.

Carol Everett, the author of *Blood Money*, tells the story of her troubled life that included sexual promiscuity and several short-lived relationships. When she had her first abortion, it caused her a great deal of emotional pain. Over time however, she became so desensitized to the taking of innocent life that she actually became a manager of an abortion clinic. She estimates 35,000 unborn children were aborted in her facilities. It was only through a dramatic encounter with the life-changing power and forgiveness of Jesus Christ that she regained her moral sensitivities. Today, she is an outspoken advocate of protecting unborn life.

Abortion isn't the only form of disconnecting that can occur. As a contributing editor to a magazine for pastors, I have heard over the years tragic stories of sexual promiscuity among pastors. A youth pastor, for example, had sexual relations in the church library with girls from his youth group even though he was married and had a family.

For him to do that required a certain "disconnect" from those who loved and trusted him the most. He had to shut down his feelings toward his wife and children. He had to switch off his pastoral concern for the young people he was supposed to care for. He had to deaden himself to the trust placed in him by the congregation. When his promiscuity was discovered, it cost him his marriage, family, and career.

Promiscuity desensitizes people to the pain they create for others. Over time we feel less and less concern, empathy, and love toward other people. They become objects, not individuals. But again, the possibility of restoration and healing is possible through the grace of God.

In his outstanding book *Tender Love: God's Gift of Sexual Intimacy* Bill Hybels tells the story of a man he calls John. John spent years involved in various sexual addictions and affairs. He had a fling with a woman he met at a bowling alley simply because she reminded him of a pin-up poster he had seen as a teenager. His marriage tottered on the brink of divorce.

During his brief affair with his "fantasy lover" he went to church. There he heard something he had waited to hear all his life: "You matter to God, no matter what." John believed that message and placed his faith in Christ. He also took a number of important steps. He confessed his sexual sins to his spouse. He received her forgiveness. He faced the consequences of his sin.

"After years of struggle," Hybels writes, "he is united in heart, mind, body, and soul with his wife, whom he once almost divorced. He eventually found in her a human incarnation of what he wanted most: unconditional love. He has stopped the affairs, the pornography, the masturbation, the endless cycle of destruction.…

"'I have the joy of making love to my wife,' the man now says. 'I have the joy of intimacy, of soul-to-soul connection.' They will soon celebrate their twenty-fifth anniversary."[4]

If we have had sexual partners in our past, God can recover our ability to connect with our spouses. The process requires confession, repentance, and facing the consequences of our past behavior, but the rewards of freedom and intimacy are well worth the struggle.

3. We need to become reconnected to God.

Sarah had spent years having affairs with married men. Her own marriages had all ended in tragedy or divorce. After her fourth marriage collapsed, she decided to give up on marriage and simply date married men.

When friends invited her to church, she was frightened. Reluctantly she went with them however. When the pastor invited people to come forward and pray at the altar if they had special needs, she froze. She wanted to go down, but she was terrified. She instinctively sensed that God knew all her secrets. The last thing in the world she wanted to do was to meet him face to face.

What Sarah didn't realize is that we don't have to clean up our act to earn God's love. His love is unconditional. We are saved by grace through faith. But if our actions are disrupting our relationship, then we need to stop what we're doing. We need to confess our sins and let God restore us to himself.

Some of you might be thinking, "But it's too late. I've messed things up too badly. God could never forgive me. He'd never take me back." Before you convince yourself you are beyond God's love, listen to this story.

Perhaps the most despicable job in the late eighteenth century was to be a captain of a slave ship. Innocent men and women were dragged from their villages in shackles and herded into the holds of ships. Those who didn't go mad from their captivity and the voyage often died of disease in the rancid conditions. Several deliberately jumped overboard to their deaths.

Captains and crew members took advantage of the female slaves and satisfied their sexual appetites as they wished. Among such individuals was a man named John Newton. He had made numerous voyages as a slave trader. He knew what it was like to inspect the ship's hold each morning and order the dead bodies thrown to the sharks.

His life of cruelty and sexual exploitation had left him disconnected from others and God in a profound fashion. But when he was nearly killed in an accident at sea, he cried out to God and discovered there was a God in heaven. Much more amazing, this God actually loved him and desired a relationship with him.

To make a long story short, John Newton experienced a spiritual birth and changed profoundly. He became a chaplain to the Queen of England and wrote one of the world's most loved hymns, "Amazing Grace." As you read a portion of that hymn, think how it applies to God's desire to reconnect with us: "Amazing grace, how sweet the sound, that saved a wretch like me. I once was lost, but now am found, was blind, but now I see. 'Twas grace that taught my heart to fear, and grace my fears relieved, how precious was that grace to me the hour I first believed."

CONCLUSION

Author David Seamands tells the story of one of his counselees who struggled with tremendous anger and perfectionism. His internal unrest was destroying his relationship with his wife, who didn't have a clue what was wrong. Finally, when things reached the breaking point, he confessed he had had a sexual relationship during a tour of duty overseas. Though the war had ended decades earlier, the battle wounds remained fresh in his soul.

As he came to understand God's forgiveness, where Christ takes both the guilt and penalty for our sinful behaviors and asks only that we accept his offer of grace, the man found peace. It was as if the part of him he had left behind returned from a distant continent. He was free to give himself to his wife again.[5]

Christ wants to do that same work in every marriage divided and diminished by past sexual partners. One spouse, one bond, one relationship until death is his formula for enjoying the best that marriage and sex can offer. His desire is to connect us with ourselves, with our spouses, and with God.

That's amazing. That's grace.

Chapter Ten

THE TRIAL WAS AN ERROR:

The Anticlimax of Premarital Sex

The night Raymond and Angela got married they didn't make love. Instead, Raymond, being tired, fell asleep. While Angela had hoped for a memorable romantic experience, for Raymond it was no big deal. Why not? Because it was no new deal, at least not in terms of their sexual experiences together.

Raymond and Angela had lived together in Idaho for over three years prior to the wedding. So while their Christmas wedding was special in terms of guests, presents, and a beautiful reception, what followed was a big yawn for Raymond, which is precisely the last sound he made before he drifted off to sleep. Angela was left wearing an expensive negligee and was—to paraphrase an old cliché—all dressed up with no one to know.

Apart from the anticlimax of the honeymoon, a couple who has engaged in premarital sex is at risk. The aftereffects of having sex before marriage don't disappear when you say "I do." Until we recognize it for the mistake it was, both in terms of defrauding one another and offending the moral character of God, it will subtly continue to corrode our marriages and the quality of our sexual relationships.

THE GROWING HABIT OF COHABITING

The Chicago study discovered a significant change in the partnering process in American society. A generation or two ago the overwhelming majority of adult Americans waited until marriage to experience sexual intimacy with their mates. Now the typical pattern of partnering goes like this. First, teenagers experience affection or love and sex with numerous partners. Then, as they reach their early twenties, they move in together. If the relationship doesn't last, the cycle starts over with another person. If the relationship does continue, it usually results in marriage.

The statistics tell the story of the changes that have occurred in our society in the last forty years. Ninety-three percent of the women born between 1933 and 1942 married without previously living with their partners. Of those women 90 percent were virgins or had intercourse only with the man they eventually married. But of the women born between 1963 and 1974 only 36 percent married without first living with their future spouses. For men the figure stands at 34 percent. That means that today almost two-thirds of all adults enter into a cohabiting relationship before marriage.[1]

According to some voices in our society that's a good thing. People are getting to know each other to see if they're compatible. This cautious approach should cut down on the tragic divorce rate that has devastated the last generation, they speculate. Those who do get married can be certain they are right for each other.

But is that the result of cohabiting before marriage? As we'll see later, it has exactly the opposite effect.

But Aren't We Different?

I can almost hear people reading these figures and saying to themselves, "Okay, that's what's going on in our society, but Christians aren't behaving like that."

Unfortunately, the spirit of the age seems to have invaded the church. The idea that Conservative Protestants, for example, are behaving differently than the rest of the culture is largely a myth, according to the Chicago research study.[2] While no doubt countless believers do maintain chaste and pure lives prior to marriage, their number is smaller than one would expect.

When the pollsters asked people who identified themselves as Conservative Protestants, "How many sex partners have you had in the last twelve months and since age eighteen?" their answers turned out to be almost identical to mainline Protestants, Catholics, and Jewish adherents. For example, 70 percent of Conservative Protestants said they had only one sexual partner in the last twelve months. But 14 percent said they had two to four lovers in the last year, and 3 percent reported five or more partners. Catholic and Jewish believers reported a higher percentage of monogamous relationships (71 percent and 75 percent respectively) in the last year.[3]

Statistics didn't get much better when Conservative Protestants were asked how many sex partners they have had since age eighteen. Only 33 percent said they had only one partner or none, while another 30 percent had been with two to four partners, 20 percent reported five to ten partners, 10 percent said they had ten to twenty lovers, and 7 percent reported twenty-one or more lovers.[4]

Those who described themselves as some "other religion," presumably Muslims, Buddhists, etc., had significantly fewer sex partners than did Conservative Protestants. Forty-five percent of this group reported having had only one partner or none since age eighteen, compared to the 33 percent of Conservative Protestants.

What does all this data mean? A significant percentage of Christians are trying to build marriages on the foundation of numerous previous sexual partners and premarital sexual experiences with their spouses.

THE GHOST OF OUR SEXUAL PAST IN OUR SEXUAL PRESENT

"So what if we did make some sexual mistakes before we were married? We're doing okay today. Why not just let the past be the past?" It's a fair question. But unless we address our premarital sexual errors, they are going to return in subtle and often disguised ways to hinder our ability to achieve true sexual intimacy and fulfillment in our marriage relationships.

But why? How could a few months of cohabiting or a few instances of sexual intercourse end up being so hazardous to the health of a marriage?

To begin, there is no such thing as a trial marriage, any more than there are trial births or deaths. Marriage is one of those incredible experiences that cannot be cloned outside the real thing.

A "trial marriage" is a contradiction in terms. By definition marriage is an exclusive, lifetime, permanent commitment. How can something temporary, nonbinding, and open ended be considered a test of something that's just the opposite? It's like trying to convince a group of Minnesotans that winter is actually a trial summer. Those brave souls of the North would check you for signs of hypothermia dementia.

Trial marriages also create distrust. When couples say, "We just want to see if we're compatible before we get married," what they're really saying is, "We have doubts about each other as future partners. And we want a quick and easy way out of this if we don't like it."

Can you see what uncertainty does to sexual intimacy? It hangs a big question mark over the bed. "Is today the last time we'll make love? What if my partner meets someone more interesting? If I don't please or perform up to standards, is this relationship over?"

The reason married sex is so superior to "trial sex" is that the questions which plague cohabiting couples have already been settled. "No, this isn't the last time we're going to have sex. Lord willing, we'll spend decades getting to know one another. No, we don't have to worry about other partners because we vowed to be faithful to our marriage partner. No, it doesn't matter if I don't perform up to standards this time because performance isn't the basis of our relationship."

Can you imagine getting into an airliner, settling back into your seat, taxiing for takeoff, then hearing the pilot say over the intercom, "Folks, I'm Captain Headwind. I'll be your pilot today—just as long as you meet my standards as passengers. If you get too demanding, too impolite, or if we merely get tired of serving you, the flight crew and I plan to bail out. We're on this flight only as long as we feel like it. Our commitment to land this plane and bring you safely to your destination is based solely on our feelings toward you. Now just sit back and enjoy the flight."

I don't know about you, but I'd be a nervous wreck until I felt the wheels touch down. How could I relax and enjoy the friendly skies when at any moment I might look out my window and see the white puff of the pilot's parachute opening?

That's what's wrong with trial marriages. It's impossible to abandon ourselves to the love of another person at night when his [or her] closet could be empty in the morning.

HOOKED ON THE THRILL OF THE FORBIDDEN

Another problem with cohabiting is what author Roger Hillerstrom calls the "illicit trap."[5] When a couple is raised within the church to believe that premarital sex is wrong, doing something forbidden or "illicit" creates a certain sense of danger or excitement, which adds adrenaline or stimulus to the sexual act. But once the couple marries, the "danger" or "naughtiness" of the sexual act is gone, making it less exciting and more routine by comparison.

To get the old "zing" back, couples may turn to other illicit behaviors, including pornography, extramarital sex, or even partner swapping. Some couples even get to the point they can't enjoy sex unless they do something "forbidden" or risqué. What a shame. They have learned to associate something beautiful, wholesome, and intimate with something immoral, unacceptable, and illicit. In the process they've diminished the potential of a perfectly fulfilling sex life.

RIGGING THE JURY AGAINST US

Another problem with cohabiting before marriage is that it rigs the jury against our future stability. Couples who lived together before marriage are divorcing at a higher rate than those who did not.

The Rockford Institute reports that "35 percent [of those who cohabited] can be expected to have terminated their first marriage before fifteen years, compared with only nineteen percent among those who did not cohabit before marriage."[6] Another study found that the longer a couple cohabited before marriage the higher their discontentment with the relationship and the possibility of divorce.[7] All of this data flies in the face of the conventional wisdom that living together before marriage creates a more stable and permanent relationship afterwards.

THE MALE GUILT TRAP

Yet another negative impact of sexual experience before marriage can be guilt and anger. As Chuck Swindoll pointed out in his fine book *Strike the Original Match,* the husband often carries guilt while the wife may deal with her anger.

The guilt the male carries usually stems from knowing he defrauded his future wife. He took something from her that didn't belong to him, at least not yet, and he did it not out of love but selfish desires. Remember the reason most men gave for their first intercourse? According to the Chicago study it wasn't love, affection, or commitment but curiosity and a readiness for sex. They had a need they wanted fulfilled, not a commitment they wanted cemented.

Perhaps years later a husband recognizes his selfish actions for what they were. The result is a sense of guilt and shame, sometimes well hidden. The feelings may even manifest themselves as a lack of sexual interest because he associates guilt with sex. (Associating guilt with sex is an almost certain way to kill or squelch desire.) The husband doesn't feel free to love his wife as God intended, and all the wife knows is that this hot lover has turned cold. But the reasons behind this cooling may be hidden from both of them.

The husband may also wrestle with guilt feelings because he knows he fell short in a basic task given him by God. He was to present his bride unblemished on their wedding day. Ephesians, chapter five, describes that unique male task: "Husbands, love your wives, just as Christ loved the church and gave himself up for her to make her holy, cleansing her by the washing with water through the word, and to present her to himself as a radiant church, without stain or wrinkle or any other blemish, but holy and blameless" (5:25–27).

The same comparison between an unblemished bride and the church is found twice in the book of Revelation: "Let us rejoice and be glad and give him glory! For the wedding of the Lamb has come, and his bride has made herself ready. Fine linen, bright and clean, was given to her to wear. (Fine linen stands for the righteous acts of the saints.)" (19:7–8; cf. 21:9).

Just as Christ has prepared a beautiful, bright, and clean bride for himself in the church, so men are to assume their role of keeping the relationship with their future brides pure and unstained. But when they pressure their future mates to satisfy their own sexual appetites, they have effectively surrendered that role. While women are held accountable for their sexual decisions and behavior, men are responsible for supporting their fiancées' desire for purity. When they don't, they are guilty of profound negligence.

So the reason a husband who was sexually active with his wife before marriage often struggles with guilt is because he is guilty. He infringed on his role as lover, preserver, and protector of his future wife's purity. He was supposed to act toward her as Christ acts toward the church, and he didn't.

A SENSE OF BETRAYAL

If the husband feels guilty, why does the wife feel angry? I think it's due to a sense of betrayal because I believe women display a natural trust in the man they love.

You see their investment of trust in relationships that go bad. How many teenage women have surrendered their virginity to a young man, only to be devastated later when he breaks up with them? "But he said he loved me," they cry.

Women, who tend to view sex in terms of relationship, affection, and commitment, often have a difficult time believing their husbands were simply using sex to satisfy their desires, not to express undying love. They trusted their future husbands, and although they might have wanted to save themselves for marriage, they perhaps gave in rather than hurt their feelings. Or perhaps the men simply wore down their will. Later the wives are angry that they were pressured to make that choice.

Worse yet, their future husbands may have forced them to do something sexual they didn't want to do. The Chicago study revealed 22 percent of all women say they have been forced by a man to do something sexual they did not want to do. Of that group of women, 46 percent say that man was someone they were in love with, while another 9 percent say it was their spouses.[8]

For women who regret being sexually active before marriage, insult is added to injury if their husbands later lose sexual interest in them. Not only did they give away something they regret, now their husbands seem bored or disinterested. It was all such a waste.

The final reason a woman may struggle with anger over her premarital sexual experiences is that she knows it was wrong. She is left with the burden of guilt we all carry when we have failed the moral law of God. One common reaction to a sense of guilt is to get angry and blame someone else for our behavior. If her husband did pressure her to become sexually active, she may be blaming him. Or, if she initiated the sexual experience, she may be angry that he wasn't strong enough to say no.

In any case the combination of unresolved guilt and anger can become toxic in a relationship. Intimacy shrivels, arguments escalate, and love dies. Even if the aftereffects are comparatively mild, a couple needs to honestly examine the impact of their premarital sexual activity.

THE WAY BACK TO HEALTH AND HEALING

For Christmas one year we bought our son a new aquarium. It contained everything we needed to set up a fully functioning, well-filtered, ecologically balanced environment for three goldfish. Once we had unwrapped and set up the filter tubes, lights, gravel, artificial plants and thermometer, it was time to add the final ingredient—water.

That seemed simple enough. Just go to the sink and fill a pitcher and start pouring. But wait. The owner at the pet store had warned us to dechlorinate the tap water before the fish were thrown in. So I picked up a bottle of "De-Chlor" and read the label on the back. "Add one drop per gallon of water," it said. "Save your fish from suffering agony or death due to chlorine."

How fascinating. Even though the water from our sink looks clear and pure, it contains an invisible chemical that will slowly, painfully, and inevitably destroy the creatures we are trying to preserve. It's much the same with premarital sexual involvement. It adds an unseen and undetected element to a couple's relational and sexual environment. Unless it's neutralized, it can cause pain, agony, and even the death of the very thing we are trying to preserve—our marriage and sexual intimacy.

So how do we "de-chlor" our sexual past?

FOUR SPIRITUAL REMEDIES

Roger Hillerstrom, a marriage therapist and author of the book *Intimate Deception,* offers four spiritual steps for dealing with past sexual mistakes:

1. Agree that you have violated God's standards. Nothing can change until you take responsibility for your part in the behavior. Call it sin; don't blame anyone else.

2. Choose to believe God's promise of forgiveness. The penalty for your sin was paid in full at Calvary. You need only to lay claim to it.

3. Choose to forgive yourself. Don't buy into guilt trips. If God has forgiven you, you are forgiven. Forgiving yourself means accepting your humanness and agreeing that Christ did the whole job on the cross. There is no more to add to it by your own suffering or self-pity.

4. Decide to make a change. Remember that healthy, growing, fulfilling relationships don't happen by accident. They are the result of decisions, commitment, and labor.[9]

In the final analysis only the blood of Jesus Christ can remove the toxins of our past sexual sins.

I read a beautiful story in the book *Fearfully and Wonderfully Made* by Philip Yancey and Paul Brand that illustrates this principle with fresh power. Several hundred years ago when smallpox was still a scourge in the world, the deadly disease had spread to South America. In the area of what is Colombia today, hundreds of thousands of people faced the dark specter of disfigurement and death.

In Spain medical doctors were experimenting with the concept of a vaccine. They had observed that humans who were exposed to serum drawn from cowpox (a disease harmless to humans) did not contract smallpox. But that offered little hope for the people in South America. The cycle of cowpox lasted only ten days to two weeks, and it took several months to cross the ocean.

Then someone suggested a bold plan. What if volunteers agreed to act as hosts to the cowpox virus? What if they voluntarily were infected with the disease? Just before the disease ran its ten-day course in one person, the serum could be drawn and used to infect the next person. That way the serum could be kept alive during the ocean crossing.

Nearly a dozen boys from an orphanage in Spain volunteered. They set sail for Colombia with the hopes and lives of countless thousands resting on their frail bodies.

The end of the story is marvelous. They reached Colombia just as the last boy's infection ran its course. The doctors hurriedly extracted serum from the boy's arm, infected others, then headed off into the countryside to begin the vaccination process. The bold, desperate plan worked.

Because those young men were willing to risk their lives and carry in their bodies the cowpox virus, an entire nation was saved. Today a statue in Colombia honors their selfless act.

Because Christ unselfishly allowed himself to be infected with the virus of our sin, he can save us from its deadly effects. His finished work on the cross is the only, and final, hope we have to remedy our past. But it requires that we place our complete trust in his death and resurrection. Then, for perhaps the first time in years, or in our lifetime, we can know true peace and freedom.

Couples need to bring their premarital sexual experiences to the cross and allow God's grace to remove the stigma, guilt, and anger they produced. When Christ forgives our sins, they are completely forgiven. The last words of Christ on the cross were, "It is finished." That phrase can also be translated, "It is paid." In the Greek language the phrase was in the perfect tense, meaning our sins were paid to perfection. We aren't partially forgiven; we are perfectly forgiven.

THE INTIMACY REPAIR KIT

But besides these spiritual steps repair work also needs to be done in the relational, emotional, and intimacy departments. For this, Hillerstrom offers five important suggestions.[10]

First, he says, couples need to realize they developed some subtle, unhealthy patterns early in their sexual relationship. Emotional guardedness and distrust slipped into the relationship because they were engaging in an act of vulnerability without lifelong commitment. Even if they weren't aware of it, they held back something of themselves just in case it didn't work out.

It was "almost" sex. They could almost trust each other. They could almost give themselves unreservedly. They could almost believe it would last. The "almost" habit the couple fell into now needs to go. That process begins by both partners realizing their early habits were destructive to God's design of openness, trust, and giving in married sex.

Second, both partners need to commit themselves before God to sort out the complications the early sexual activity created. That can be an intimidating, even fearful, process to begin. But, as I said earlier, the only way out is through.

There are some drawers in our house I rarely or never open. I purposely stay away from them because they are filled with old papers, canceled bills, and general clutter. I find it stressful to sit down and try to sort out what I should keep and what I should throw away. But if I want to clean house, that's what I have to do.

The same is true for a marriage. We have to make a conscious decision to open the old files and sort through the issues that have cluttered our lives. The very decision to face the past and work through it is a significant step toward healing.

Third, Hillerstrom suggests couples educate themselves about healthy communication patterns. If ordinary conflicts regularly escalate into dramatic and intense showdowns, if the smallest criticism elicits from either spouse a major defensive reaction, or if one partner can't deal with a tension in the marriage without being wounded, it's time to learn a different way of communicating.

The couple may have short-circuited the process of learning to talk in a healthy way to each other because of their early sexual involvement. If they spent more time in bed than they did on the phone, they probably missed the "thousand hours" of conversation needed to bond properly. In order to learn to communicate, a couple may need to go back to the "voice-to-voice stage" in the twelve-step process of bonding author Dr. Donald Joy outlines.[11] Fortunately all of us can learn to discard defensive, angry reactions in favor of open, listening patterns.

Fourth, couples need consciously to work on straightening out the "double messages" regarding their commitment to the relationship. With their bodies they said they were committing themselves to the other person. Yet, because they hadn't taken the step of getting married, their actions sent the message "I still want the option of getting out of this relationship."

Hillerstrom says it's important now to affirm regularly one's love and commitment to the marriage, especially when things get rough. A person needs to say with words and actions, "Even though we may be having our problems right now, I'm not leaving. I'll be here today, tomorrow, and for the rest of my life."

Finally, if there are some issues the couple just can't get past, they should seek the help of a counselor. The path toward healing may be too arduous and complicated for two people to walk it alone. Don't be afraid to ask for help.

As someone has observed, "Pain is inevitable, misery is optional." Although we may experience pain in working through our marriage problems, we don't have to live in misery. We can make progress. We can build healthy relationships. We can start over. If anger and guilt have been unseen but consistent houseguests, it's time to show them the door. We can do that with the help of a qualified, caring, Christian pastor or counselor.

ONLY AS PUBLIC AS THE SIN

One word of caution. There's no need for a person to broadcast his sin or past to the entire world. While some people may be tempted to do public penance, it's often unwise. In most cases no one but God needs to know the details of the past sin.

A wise college professor of mine offered some excellent advice in this matter. He told our class the story of a student who came into his office to confess a sin, presumably a moral failure.

Just as the student began to offer the details of his story, the professor stopped him. "My friend," said the professor, "confession should be as public as the sin, and no more."

Earning forgiveness for past sin—sexual or otherwise—is contrary to the doctrine of the sacrificial atonement of Christ. "For it is by grace you have been saved, through faith—and this not from yourselves, it is the gift of God—not by works, so that no one can boast" (Ephesians 2:8–9).

While sharing the weight of our past with a counselor or pastor can help lift it off our shoulders, we don't need to tell everyone. It may only complicate, or perhaps even overwhelm, people who aren't prepared to deal with it. If a public confession is called for, usually a wise pastor or counselor will recognize that fact and offer important guidelines for doing it in an appropriate manner. In every case we should consult a wise, godly, and experienced pastor or counselor before making such a decision.

Ultimately we must remember there is only one Person able to bear our sin, who knows every sordid detail and has taken on himself the punishment we deserve. "But he was pierced for our transgressions, he was crushed for our iniquities; the punishment that brought us peace was upon him, and by his wounds we are healed" (Isaiah 53:5).

CONCLUSION

So how can you begin the healing process in your marriage today? Let me suggest that individually, or perhaps together, you pray this prayer: "Father in heaven, I thank you that you know our entire life story. You gave us the gift of one another, but we misused and took advantage of that gift. I confess to you the sexual sin committed before our marriage. On the basis of Christ's finished work on the cross, I ask your forgiveness. I believe your promise that, 'If we confess our sins, you are faithful and just and will forgive us our sins and purify us from all unrighteousness.'

"Please Lord, let the distrust, the double messages, the guilt, and the anger be removed from our relationship. Let them be replaced with forgiveness, trust, and a lifelong commitment to one another. Let every aspect of our marriage, including our sexual relationship, glorify you and fulfill the purpose for which you brought us together. I thank you that you are a God rich in mercy and overflowing with love. We now receive and rejoice in your forgiveness. In the name of Christ, we pray. Amen."

Chapter Eleven

RECOVERING FROM VISUAL ADULTERY

I had just finished speaking at a conference when a woman asked if Cheryl and I would speak with her for a moment. Once we were off in a corner, she thanked us for warning couples to keep pornography from entering their marriage. Then she shared how her life had become a nightmare as the result of her husband's insistence they act out pornographic images he had seen in magazines and videos. "There were days I would just start shaking uncontrollably at work, and I had no idea why," she said. He threatened to kill her if she told anyone of his habit. Finally she fled the United States to escape his abuse. Now they are divorced, and she is back in the country, but the memories of those terrifying days still linger.

Not every marriage suffers to that extent from the influence of pornography, but inevitably a price will be paid—either in diminished interest or intimacy in sex, or in outright cruelty and abuse.

Is the problem widespread in our culture? According to the Chicago study 41 percent of men and 16 percent of women in America have spent money on at least one of the following in the last twelve months: X-rated movies or videos, a visit to a club with nude or seminude dancers, sexually explicit videos or magazines, sex toys, sex phone numbers, or other autoerotic devices.[1]

There's no question that pornography has invaded millions of homes in America. Is there a way back? Can a couple regain sexual wholeness and satisfaction in a marriage that's been poisoned by pornography? Fortunately, the answer is yes. Unfortunately, it isn't easy.

A FOOTHOLD BECOMES A STRANGLEHOLD

Perhaps the most widely read article in the history of *Leadership Journal,* a magazine for pastors, was published anonymously. It's the true story of a pastor who had gone to a city on the East Coast for a speaking engagement. Bored and alone, he wandered one evening into the "combat zone" of the city. The streets were filled with cheap bars and restaurants that featured nude dancers. He was curious as to what he had missed, living as a respectable pastor, so with no one watching he walked into a bar that featured a former beauty queen doing a striptease.

Being unfamiliar with alcoholic beverages, he ordered straight whiskey, as he had seen in Westerns. He downed the shot glass with a single gulp and nearly choked. But soon the combination of hard liquor and forbidden excitement began to take hold.

He watched as other men gave the performers money in return for special favors. He fumbled through his pockets, then handed one of the women a ten dollar bill. His sense of moral restraint and self-control had been seduced by the sweet promises of lust and liquor.

When he finally stumbled out of the bar into the night, something inside him had changed. He had experienced an intoxicating evening that had left him feeling more alive than he had felt in a long time.

He consoled his uneasy conscience with the thought this was only a one-time experience. But he soon discovered otherwise. A seemingly irresistible force drew him toward the soft-core pornography available on newsstands. Before long he was not just leafing through the magazines but was buying them and hiding them from his wife. The sensation he had experienced that first night in the bar tingled back to life. He discovered he not only enjoyed these materials but now he needed them. Curiosity led to attraction, attraction to obsession, and finally, obsession to addiction.

At church he continued to carry on his pastoral duties, but on the side he frequented pornographic bookstores, adult video galleries, and bars that featured live sex acts. Not coincidentally, his sexual relationship with his wife began to suffer. Eventually it all but disappeared. Pornography had become the center of his life.

However, he had not lost all his moral bearings. He knew what he was doing was wrong, even self-destructive, but he couldn't stop. He developed both a hate and a love for pornography. In his more honest moments he knew his life was out of control.

Realizing his career and marriage were in serious jeopardy, he summoned the courage to schedule an appointment with an older pastor. As the day drew near, he could hardly believe the things he would need to confess—or the person he had become.

He felt both fear and relief as their appointment began. The older pastor was an individual he had deeply admired and respected for years. He was a powerful preacher, a successful evangelist, a godly man—everything the young pastor wanted to become.

After an initial exchange of pleasantries, the young pastor confessed his sins. He told the entire sordid tale—the first night at the bar with nude dancers, the need for soft-core pornography and then for more obscene and hard-core materials, the terrible guilt, the self-hatred, his deteriorating marriage, the fear he was losing control of his life.

At first the older, wiser gentleman said nothing, but simply listened. Then tears formed in the eyes of the confidant. Soon the man's face was contorted with pain, and he began to sob. Before long, he was doubled over, convulsing with anguish. The younger pastor was moved by this older gentleman's apparent grief over his sin.

When the older man had regained a measure of composure, he reached into his pocket and produced several slips of paper which he handed, trembling, to the younger man. They were doctor's prescriptions.

"I carry several venereal diseases in my body," sobbed the older man.

"What?" said the astonished young pastor.

"That's right," he said between sobs. "I have some for which there is no cure."

The older man then began to pour out his own story. When he was much younger, he had fallen into the same trap of lust-addictive behaviors. He was now about to lose everything—his integrity, his marriage, and his health.

The younger man sat stunned, groping for words. He never would have dreamed, not in a thousand years, that this gentleman could be a prisoner, a casualty, of his sexual appetites.

"Get help now before it's too late," the older pastor pleaded between sobs.

That encounter shook the young pastor to the core. He

realized he could not experience the wholeness and satisfaction he desperately desired if he continued to let his sexual desires, rather than his moral will, guide his life. He began a serious effort to break free from his addiction to pornography.[2]

TAKING US PLACES WE NEVER WANTED TO GO

Though printed pornography didn't exist in ancient times, we can see how King David and King Herod were influenced by visual lust—as David watched Bathsheba bathe and Herod watched Herodias's daughter perform in a provocative manner. In both cases lust led to murder. David had Bathsheba's husband, Uriah, killed, while Herod ordered John the Baptist beheaded at the request of Herodias's daughter.

The same voyeurism that motivated David and Herod to act in irrational and violent ways thrives in pornography today. Modern studies link the use of pornography with violence against women and children. Besides the attorney general's report on pornography in the 1980s, which suggested a strong correlation between pornography and violence, scores of women personally testify to it each year. Carefully controlled research studies also show pornography lowers the commitment males feel to the institution of marriage.[3]

Consider the true story of Pat Haas. "'[When I] began dating Bob [pseudonym], he seemed warm, affectionate,' she recalls.... Then, over a period of time, he became increasingly sadistic and even tortured Haas. If she resisted, he beat her and threatened to kill her. She had become his 'sexual servant,' Haas says; she had no will of her own."

Haas charges Bob's ideas were modeled after a sadomasochistic movie from his extensive collection of pornographic videos. He would play the movie on the VCR, freeze framing the tape whenever a particular activity interested him, and say, "I want you to do that."[4]

Haas's story appeared in the *Ladies Home Journal* in an article that went on to document the research done by Wendy Stock, Ph.D., an assistant professor of psychology at Texas A & M. Her studies show that men prefer pornographic material that is "dehumanizing toward women." The article also pointed out research conducted by Neil Malamuath, Ph.D., head of the communications department at the University of Michigan, who concludes that messages which suggest sexual violence against women is acceptable "do change attitudes for some men."[5]

But despite these known facts, many in our culture still argue that viewing pornography is no threat to anyone's safety or well-being. Some even insist it's a constitutional right protected under the "freedom of the press" clause.

The Stone Temple Pilots, a popular rock group, produced a video entitled "That Sex Type Thing," which portrays a young woman in an empty warehouse. A masculine figure, with muscles rippling and sweat beading on his skin, stands ready to gratify his desires. The message is quite clear: rape is a sexually gratifying experience for men (and possibly an experience women secretly crave).

IT ADDS A LITTLE SIZZLE TO OUR MARRIAGE

Many couples argue that a hot video or a racy magazine can actually bring steam back into a lukewarm love life by firing up the imagination and intensifying desire. Tracy Cabot, a therapist and author, claims, "If my husband and I like a particular movie, we buy it. I enjoy the fact it's a little naughty; it gives us new ideas. I make no apologies."[6]

Is that true? Does pornography improve a couple's sex life? In the short term it may add intensity, but in the long run it destroys the very fabric of the relationship.

Why is that?

IT LEADS TO VISUAL ADULTERY.

Let's go back to a basic fact of life. Men are sexually aroused by what they see much more than women are. When a man uses pornography during sexual intercourse, his mind, his emotions, and his passions are directed toward the image on the screen or in the magazine. In his imagination he is having sex with an anonymous stranger, not his wife.

So when a woman allows her husband to use pornography during their sexual encounters, she's actually allowing him to have sex with someone else. If he responds with more intensity, it's because he's involved with someone new, someone other than her. I call that "visual adultery."

Let me ask a pertinent question. How many wives would prefer their husbands be sexually aroused by some other woman, then come to bed with them? The very notion is disgusting. But that's what pornography is all about. If we think otherwise, we're terribly naive.

IT LEADS TO DAMAGING COMPARISONS.

Whether it's *Playboy* magazine or an R-rated movie, the lighting, the makeup, and the angle of the camera are designed to create maximum attraction for the male viewer. That puts the average wife, perhaps exhausted from a day of work or caring for children, in a difficult situation. As time and age take their toll, wives find it increasingly difficult to compete with the young nymphs that publishers and moviemakers glamorize.

When men compare their wives to these artificial goddesses, they may lose some of the desire for their wives. As the pastor in the *Leadership Journal* article confessed, his sex life with his wife dwindled as his obsession with pornography grew.

That's no coincidence. Human nature is such that a new experience almost always appears more exciting to us than one we've experienced over and over again. That's why viewing the nude body of someone you've never met is so titillating, and pornography distributors understand that. Over time the male who uses pornography finds his own wife's body too routine to provide excitement and satisfaction. When that happens, the relationship is headed for serious trouble.

IT DESTROYS THE PAIR BOND.

One of the important steps in bonding is "eye to body," as Donald Joy describes it.[7] When a man regularly views other females, that bond is weakened. He finds himself sexually, and often emotionally, engaged by this person he sees on paper or on the television screen. His fantasies and desires are redirected.

Perhaps an analogy will help. Let's say the sexual bonding process is like putting masking tape on your arm. The first time you do it, the tape sticks tightly. In marriage that tape is intended to stick for a lifetime. But if you take that piece of tape and put it on and tear it off over and over again, it will come off a bit easier and hurt less each time. Repeat the process four or five times, or thirty or fifty times, and it's doubtful the tape will bond to you at all.

The same thing happens when a male visually bonds with a

different woman time after time after time. Eventually he has trouble being bonded to anyone at all, particularly his wife. As their pair bond is weakened, if not destroyed, genuine intimacy and sexual fulfillment become virtually impossible.

THE LAW OF DIMINISHING RETURNS WORKS AGAINST US.

Few experts dispute that pornography can lead to a progressive addiction that requires more and more erotic material to achieve the same result. Whereas *Playboy* once was enough to generate steam in a relationship, now increasingly hard-core materials are needed to achieve the same effect. In some cases men then turn to materials that feature violence and sadomasochism to satisfy their desires.

As the taste in pornography turns toward more abnormal materials, husbands frequently demand that their wives engage in these perverted acts. What was once meant to bring joy and satisfaction to a couple now produces fear, loathing, and often violence.

Another woman told us that after years of being married to a man addicted to pornography, she now fears every sexual encounter they have. She suffers from nervous exhaustion and finds it difficult to function normally, either in everyday life or in bed.

Some might argue, "But that's an extreme case. All we do as a couple is watch a dirty movie together once in a while." While that may be true now, I doubt it will be true five or ten years from now. I predict by that time a couple either will have abandoned pornography altogether, or the materials will have become significantly worse. It's going to be one or the other.

THE ROAD TO HEALING AND FREEDOM

So how do couples recover from pornography if it's gained control over their lives and marriages?

Counselors use a number of different strategies. Many treat it as an addiction, using variations of the twelve-step approach, which includes admitting one's life is out of control, conducting a ruthless moral inventory, making restitution where necessary, and maintaining accountability to others.

Other approaches help people see the patterns they have developed that lead them to obsessive behaviors. If people see that when they get depressed they turn to pornography to feel better, alternate ways of dealing with sadness—such as prayer, calling a friend, or going out to exercise—can be utilized.

I believe for any approach to succeed we must view the primary problem in an addiction to pornography as a spiritual one. As such, it requires a spiritual answer. David, who found himself a prisoner of his own voyeuristic passions, wrote a psalm in which he confessed that his main problem was a spiritual one. A brief look at Psalm 51 shows us how he dealt with the issue and found both forgiveness and healing, and how we can do the same.

He labeled his problem as sin.

Perhaps the healthiest thing David did was to avoid rationalizing or explaining away his behavior. He said, "For I know my transgressions, and my sin is always before me. Against you, you only, have I sinned and done what is evil in your sight, so that you are proved right when you speak and justified when you judge" (51:3–4).

It is the plague of our times to label every sinful and self-destructive act an addiction. People no longer commit adultery, they are "fidelity impaired." They don't lie, they suffer from "truth deficiency syndrome." They don't covet, they simply are "contentment challenged individuals." Certainly some mental and emotional disorders deserve to be classified as obsessions or compulsions. But underneath these aberrant behaviors lies the human will, where we decide to act on a compulsion or to refuse.

I know that chocolate-covered, deep fried doughnuts are a cholesterol transgression. When I spot a bag of them on the counter, I think, "They look good, but I can't have them." Then I waver. "I know they aren't good for me.... So I'll just count how many are in the bag, but I won't actually eat one." Next, I smell to see if they're fresh. Finally I decide it won't hurt that much to tear off just one piece. "Okay," I rationalize, "since I've already eaten part of it, I might as well eat the rest. After all, who's going to want it now?"

While I may have gone through a series of emotional transitions and rationalizations before I chomp down on that first doughnut, the truth is I finally chose to eat it. And it was the wrong thing to do. I simply have to admit that.

I tend to agree with the counselors who say, "Addictive behavior is both a disease and a choice—bondage and rebellion. Therefore we want to get to the root of the disease—the trauma, pain, rejection, and poor parenting that the child received. In this, the child had no choice; he is in bondage to the sin of others. But we must face concurrently the choices the addict has made along the road—choices toward sin. If both sides of the problem aren't confronted, change is impossible."[8] David faced his lust and adulterous behavior and called it what it was— rebellion: "Against you, you only, have I sinned and done what is evil in your sight."

Couples who have fallen into the trap of using pornographic movies, videos, or magazines to heat up their sex lives need to admit the truth. They have sinned against a holy God. That recognition alone won't solve their problem, but it's the first step.

He recognized the pain his sin had created.

One of the classic symptoms of addictive behavior is denial, which is nothing less than minimizing the impact or consequences of what we've done.

We often rationalize to ourselves the reasons we become involved in pornography:

> "The human body is beautiful and meant to be enjoyed."
>
> "It creates more passion in our marriage."
>
> "It doesn't affect anyone but me, and I can take it or leave it."
>
> "We men need more stimulation than our wives can offer us."

But all such rationalizations simply mask the truth of what our sin does to ourselves and to others.

Only when we begin to admit the pain we have created for others by our sinful actions will we begin to experience the power of repentance. We cannot be forgiven for something we have not admitted. As long as we deny the impact of our behavior on others, we will most likely continue in it.

David realized his actions had resulted in the betrayal of those who trusted him, the murder of an innocent man, the compromise of an otherwise faithful wife, and eventually the death of a child.

He asked for the guilt of his sin to be removed.

I once read where a doctor in a psychiatric ward commented, "The majority of these people could go home if they actually believed they were forgiven." But guilt is not simply a neurotic emotional state. It is a real, objective, spiritual condition that an individual experiences when he has done something morally wrong.

David prayed, "Cleanse me with hyssop, and I will be clean; wash me, and I will be whiter than snow. Let me hear joy and gladness; let the bones you have crushed rejoice. Hide your face from my sins and blot out all my iniquity" (51:7–9).

A carpenter in Nevada was building a home on a windy day. He was holding a compressed-air nail gun in one hand and putting up a board with the other. When a gust of wind caught the board, he reflexively squeezed the trigger of the nail gun.

Immediately he felt a pain in his chest, and when he looked down, he saw the head of a nail protruding out of the center of his T-shirt. His co-worker ran over, took one look at him, and rushed him to the nearest emergency room. After x-rays and sonograms were taken, the doctor discovered to his horror that the man had fired a nail into his own heart. The carpenter was immediately rushed into surgery, and against all odds the surgeon was able to remove the nail and suture the wound.

In a similar sense sin lodges a nail in our hearts. If left there, it will eventually destroy us. It must be removed. But how?

That's where the work of Jesus Christ on the cross is our hope and remedy. With nails driven through his sacrificial arms, he paid the penalty for our sins. The Scriptures promise, "He forgave us all our sins, having canceled the written code, with its regulations, that was against us and that stood opposed to us; he took it away, nailing it to the cross" (Colossians 2:14).

Pornography does more than just damage our relationship with our spouses; it damages our relationship with God. The objective guilt we feel is because something has come between us and God. And only God through Christ has the ability to remove our sin and make us clean and whole once more.

He can remove the nail.

He asked for purity so he could enjoy God once more.

Remember the woman's statements earlier? "If my husband and I like a particular movie, we buy it. I enjoy the fact it's a little naughty; it gives us new ideas. I make no apologies." Her stance is at odds with David's prayer, "Create in me a pure heart, O God, and renew a steadfast spirit within me. Do not cast me from your presence or take your Holy Spirit from me" (51:10–11).

The issue isn't whether feeding lust is "naughty" or not; the issue is the price we pay in losing the ability to experience intimacy with our spouses and with God. Apparently David discovered a connection between a pure heart and experiencing the presence of God.

For an addiction to be broken in our lives, we are going to have to want something more than what we currently have. An alcoholic ultimately has to want the benefits of sobriety more than the pleasures of drunkenness. In the same way we ultimately have to see that the pleasures of purity are far more fulfilling than the titillations of lust.

When we seek purity so that we might experience God, we find that passion and romance re-enter our marriage at the same time. God isn't sitting in heaven desperately trying to keep men and women from experiencing sexual thrills and erotic delights. No, the truth is, God created us to experience both his presence and the gift of sex with our spouses on a much higher level than we can imagine. While "naughty" may be stimulating, experiencing true intimacy is incredibly electrifying. True intimacy happens through purity, and purity and pornography can't coexist. One or the other has to move out of our lives.

David affirmed his standing with God.

Imagine a house with no locks, no glass in the windows, not even a door in the doorway. That house could be burglarized or vandalized at will. That's our spiritual condition when we fail to have a relationship with Jesus Christ—we are vulnerable to spiritual attack. The same thing can also occur when we fail to recognize and affirm as believers who we are in Christ. Every deception, accusation, and temptation our adversary, the devil, can think of is thrown at us with little to resist his onslaught. The result for many people is that the devil wreaks havoc in their lives through pornography.

Notice how important it was to David that he reaffirm his standing with God. "Do not cast me from your presence, or take your Holy Spirit from me. Restore to me the joy of your salvation and grant me a willing spirit, to sustain me" (51:11–12). With the certainty of God's presence and a fresh sense of the joy of his salvation, David could survive the difficult circumstances he faced. He could again be strong in his faith.

To resist the pull of pornography, it's so important that we understand our relationship with God and our standing with Christ. Our victory, our freedom, our dignity have been secured by the finished work of Christ. His death, resurrection, and ascension into heaven have sealed our victory over any sin we might confront. Perhaps the most important spiritual principle we can use in a battle with lust and its attending addictions is this: As Christians we don't work toward victory; we work out from victory, according to author Timothy Warner.

Read carefully what Paul says in Colossians, "For in Christ all the fullness of the Deity lives in bodily form, and you have been given fullness in Christ, who is the head over every power and authority.... And having disarmed the powers and authorities, he [Christ] made a public spectacle of them, triumphing over them by the cross" (2:9–10, 15). We have in Christ the authority to slam the door shut on the deceptions, accusations, and temptations that drive us toward compulsive, self-destructive, and sinful behavior. It is not a matter of how weak or strong we are; it's entirely a matter of the authority we now carry.

When I was in sixth grade, I was elected to the safety patrol. As part of this high honor I received a white shoulder belt, a badge, and a fluorescent orange flagpole with the word "Stop" emblazoned on it. Once each morning and each afternoon I marched out to my street corner to help younger students cross busy intersections.

I remember how I felt the first time I lowered the pole and a car actually stopped. I soon discovered I could stop almost any size, shape, or weight vehicle. If a tiny Volkswagen cruised up, I could bring it to a screeching halt. If a huge, multiton garbage truck thundered down the street, all it took was my dropping the flag, and his air brakes would hiss and squeal as he was forced to halt. I could even back up five cars at a time. This was pretty heady stuff for a twelve-year-old.

But what if I had gone into the intersection without a belt, badge, or pole? What if, on my own, I had decided to stop traffic? Or what if I had decided to use my own strength to push back the cars, the vans, and the garbage trucks? My frail eighty-five pounds would have been little match for the ten-thousand-pound garbage truck on its way to the landfill. I would have been approximately the thickness of wallpaper once it had rolled over me.

The secret of my power to stop three-hundred-horsepower vehicles that crisscrossed my intersection wasn't my strength, intelligence, or personality; it was my badge. I wore a symbol of authority that other motorists were compelled to respect. The same is true of people who have placed their trust in Jesus Christ for their salvation. They are given at the moment of their conversion a badge of authority that the principalities and powers of this universe must respect.

LEARNING OUR ABCDS

I believe much of our vulnerability to temptations such as pornography is born of wrong beliefs. We accept the faulty ideas that we are stupid, unlovable, inadequate, unloved, and unworthy. To deaden this inner pain we seek anesthetics like drugs, alcohol, pornography, overeating, and other compulsive behaviors.

Some counselors refer to this as the ABCD system. First, there is an Activating event, which is interpreted by our Belief systems, causing Consequential feelings, which result in Decisive behavior.

Perhaps a boss criticizes us at work—the Activating event. Our Belief system interprets that criticism to mean, "You are a faulty, worthless person." The Consequential feelings of self-hatred and shame drive us to pick up a pornographic magazine, which temporarily anesthetizes our pain with titillating emotions. For the time being we enjoy it. But then our feelings of shame and self-hatred come back, perhaps this time even stronger because we had told ourselves we wouldn't touch pornography again. The destructive, downward cycle is at work.

So how is it broken? As counselors Hal Schell and Gary Sweeten write, "We have no control over Activating events, and Consequential feelings are caused by what we believe about events. The Decisive behavior results directly from feelings. Therefore the place to work is the Belief system."[9] We can't control what the boss says at work, or how others treat us, or even how our spouse responds to us. But we can alter our Belief system. We can line up what we believe with what the Scriptures say about us. When that happens, our Consequential feelings are going to change. Ultimately it will impact our Decisive behaviors.

THE TRUTH ABOUT WHO WE REALLY ARE

Let's begin by examining our beliefs. What do the Scriptures say about the value, dignity, and worthiness of us as believers who are born into an eternal relationship with Christ?

First of all, we are loved with an incredible, everlasting love. John 3:16 tells us, "For God so loved the world that he gave his one and only Son, that whoever believes in him shall not perish but have eternal life."

Do you feel unloved? Unworthy? Unacceptable? Well, you aren't. In fact, if you're turning to pornography to fill a love hunger in your life, I've got very good news. God can meet your need for love in a way a videocassette never can. If you ran into one of the models from *Playboy* or the latest NC-17 video, chances are she wouldn't give you the time of day. She may have taken off her clothes for the camera, but she'll never give you her heart. But God loves you so much he gave the very best he had to establish a relationship with you. "In love he predestined us to be adopted as his sons through Jesus Christ, in accordance with his pleasure and will" (Ephesians 1:4–5).

But what about those feelings of self-hatred and self-condemnation that drive you to feed lust or to seek illicit sexual excitement to ease your pain? Listen to this incredible statement: "Therefore, there is now no condemnation for those who are in Christ Jesus" (Romans 8:1). Regardless of the voices that condemn, accuse, or degrade us, God will not. As believers, he views us through Christ as if we had never sinned. Not even once. He accepts us just as we are in Christ Jesus. It's not that we don't have problems, faults, or even sin in our lives. It's that God has forgiven us of these things because of Christ's work on the cross.

In the city of Chicago we have an absurd tax collection system called tollgates. Someone had the remarkable idea that the drivers of tens of thousands of cars per hour should be stopped to look for loose change in their pockets. (I personally believe this plan was hatched in collusion with chiropractors and manufacturers of blood pressure medicine.) The resulting backup sometimes extends several miles and several hours.

One day I was following another van from our church down the tollway. When it reached the tollgate, the driver paid for both of us. As I got to the gate, the attendant waved me through. I stopped to offer the money, but he refused it. It would have been useless (even dangerous) to hold up traffic and insist the man take my toll.

In the same way our toll has already been paid by Christ. There is nothing left for us to do to earn our salvation or prove we don't deserve condemnation. When the accusing thoughts start—"You're worthless. You're sick. You're evil,"—we can respond by saying, "Not true. There is now no condemnation in Christ Jesus." In fact, Romans 6:11 tells us to "count yourselves dead to sin, but alive to God in Christ Jesus." You can't file charges against a dead person, can you?

And what of our authority in Christ? Listen to Ephesians 2:6: "And God raised us up with Christ and seated us with him in the heavenly realms in Christ Jesus." Today, as believers, we possess the same regal authority as if we were seated on the throne in heaven next to Christ himself. Such authority gives us the ability to say in the face of overpowering temptation to revert to pornography, "In the name of Christ Jesus, I refuse to give in to this." To add to your arsenal of authority, why not memorize 1 Corinthians 10:13: "No temptation has seized you except what is common to man. And God is faithful; he will not let you be tempted beyond what you can bear. But when you are tempted, he will also provide a way out so that you can stand up under it."

CONCLUSION

Brendon had been raised in a chaotic, angry home in Idaho. His stepfather actually beat him. He was just a boy when his friends set him up with an older girl, and he surrendered his innocence.

His low self-esteem, his anger at his parents, and his early, distorted sexual experiences set him up to become a pornography addict. Even though he married a beautiful woman, he had an insatiable appetite for pornography. As anger and sex in his life became mixed, he would ask his wife to follow through with his bizarre fantasies. They teetered on the brink of divorce.

But by the grace of God a pastor was able to reach out to Brendon and show him how God loved him. As Brendon caught a glimpse of what true love, acceptance, and value in Christ meant, he began to change the way he saw himself. Eventually he decided to take a radical step. He gathered up his considerable stash of pornographic materials and threw them away. The scars of Brendon's years of addiction are still evident in his family, but for the first time in his life, he is on the road to freedom.

There is no such thing as harmless pornography any more than there is harmless cocaine. Pornography, given enough time, will destroy its users. If pornography has invaded your marriage, today is the day to take one of the most important walks of your life. Take the materials—all of them—and deposit them in your garbage can. Claim your position of freedom and authority in Christ. Then make yourself accountable to a pastor, counselor, or close friend to stay free from pornography. It will be the start of the renewal of your marital sexual relationship.

Chapter Twelve

CAN YOU HEAL A BROKEN HEART?

C ome on, dear, you'll be late for soccer practice," said Molly's mother.

"I can't find my other shoe," shouted Molly down the stairwell. "Adam is always coming into my room and messing everything up. I know I put them by the door last night. I can't stand it when someone loses my things."

Karen Morrison, Molly's mother, smiled as she waited patiently for her nine-year-old daughter to find her things. Molly was a bright, creative little third grader who was hopelessly disorganized. In less than sixty seconds Molly appeared at the top of the stairs in her soccer uniform, hopping on one foot as she attempted to pull on her other shoe.

"Molly, you can put it on in the car. We need to leave right now if you want to get there on time," said Karen. "The car is running. Let's go."

"Okay, okay," Molly responded. The little girl followed her mom to the minivan with one shoe on, the other in her hand.

"Lock your door and put on your seat belt," said Karen.

"Oh, Mom," moaned Molly.

"Do as I say." Karen checked her rearview mirror and pulled out of the driveway. Her five-year-old, Adam, was playing video games at the next door neighbor's house. That would give her a chance to pick up something at the store before she had to go after Molly and before Jeff, her husband, got home. He had called and said he would be late again.

As the young mother looked again in the mirror, she noticed how sad her eyes appeared. "I need to do something with this makeup," she thought to herself. "I look dreadful."

Her expression warmed when she looked next to her and saw Molly waving her arms, rehearsing her goalie moves.

The afternoon sun was bright in Karen's eyes as she pulled onto the busy thoroughfare. "Where are my sunglasses?" she asked, reaching down into her purse to dig through the clutter. She was approaching an intersection, but the light was green.

"Mama, watch out!" cried Molly.

Out of the side of her eye Karen saw a green Honda Accord with a man and a woman in the front seat.

"What? Oh no!"

Those were the last words Karen was able to utter before the impact. The Honda shot through the red light and hit their minivan broadside. Karen heard Molly scream. The full impact of the collision pushed their vehicle across the intersection and then rolled the van over on its side. Karen was thrown against the window on her side, while Molly's door took the worst of it.

For a moment everything was quiet. Then Karen opened her eyes, in a near state of shock, and gasped. There lay Molly unconscious, her uniform stained with blood. Karen tried to move her arm, but a searing pain went from one side of her body to the other. "My baby, my baby," she moaned. Then everything went black.

≈

"Get that sliding door open!" shouted the paramedic to one of the firemen on the scene. The strong odor of gasoline filled the intersection as emergency workers scrambled to get Karen and Molly out of the vehicle.

"Base, this is Charlie Five. We have an accident with serious injuries at Clydesdale and Van Buren," said a police sergeant, leaning against his squad car.

"Roger, Charlie Five. We're alerting Henson Memorial for trauma patients," came back the voice of a female dispatcher.

The Accord had a shattered windshield and a disfigured hood and grille. Although it had been totaled in the collision, the occupants were standing next to the vehicle, talking to police.

"Those air bags saved your life, mister," said a young lieutenant.

"I know, I know," said the driver. His female companion cried as she looked at the scene across the intersection. The paramedics were strapping a little girl to a stretcher. She already had an IV tube hanging above her.

"Witnesses say you ran the red light," said the officer.

"Yeah, I guess I did," the man mumbled. "I'm sorry."

"I need to see your driver's license and insurance card."

The middle-aged man fumbled in his suit pocket for his wallet. He opened it up, and there, enclosed in a plastic protective sheet, was a picture of his wife and two children. A knife went through his stomach. He quickly grabbed the cards he was looking for and handed them to the officer. He couldn't bring himself to look in the direction of the victims.

❦

The pictures of a clown and elephant on the wall slowly came into focus. Molly tried to open her eyes, but her eyelids felt as if they were made of lead.

"Sweetheart, can you hear me?"

Molly turned her head in the direction of the voice. Next to her stood a nurse, and next to the nurse was a lady in a wheelchair.

"Mama?" whispered Molly.

"Oh, my baby," the woman said, tears in her voice.

When Molly was at last able to focus, she saw a woman with a large bandage wrapped around her head. Both her eyes were black, and one arm was in a cast. "Mama, is that you?"

"Yes, sweetheart. It's me."

"Where are we?" Molly tried to sit up but was too dizzy. She dropped her head back down on the pillow.

"Don't try to sit up, honey. Just rest."

"What happened?"

"We were in a car accident, sweetheart," said Karen. "But we're going to be fine. Mommy has a broken arm and some broken ribs, and you had a concussion, Molly."

"Am I going to die?" Molly asked, frightened.

"No, dear. You're doing great. The doctors said it's just going to take a while for you to feel better. But don't worry; Mommy's going to stay right here next to you."

"Where's Adam?" Molly asked.

"He's at grandma's house, honey. He's too young to come to visit you, but he'll call you when you're feeling better."

"Where's Daddy? I want to see my daddy." For the first time Molly was about to cry.

Karen looked up at the nurse, who shook her head no.

❦

Molly was given heavy sedatives and slept most of the next two days. She didn't remember much, except she couldn't move with the plastic tubes going into each arm.

Three nights later just after supper Karen was wheeled into Molly's room. "How are you feeling, sweetheart?" asked Karen, the bandage now removed.

"Mommy, what are those train tracks on your forehead?" Molly responded, a giggle in her voice.

"Those are stitches, dear."

"You mean like the ones we used to sew up Ruth Ann?" Ruth Ann was Molly's doll. Adam had once tried to take Ruth Ann out of the dog's mouth, and the arm had torn loose. Karen had quickly saved the day by sewing it back together.

"Yes, like Ruth Ann." Karen took a deep breath, carefully considering her next words. "Honey, someone's here who wants to see you."

"Who? Another doctor? Can you please ask him to take these tubes out? They're making my arms turn colors...."

"No, Molly. It's not a doctor."

Just then a tall man dressed in a blue sweater and khaki pants appeared at the door.

"Daddy!" screamed Molly.

The man was momentarily shaken by Molly's appearance but quickly made his way to her bedside. "My darling, my little darling," he sobbed as he held his daughter in his arms. Karen looked down and fought back tears.

"Where have you been, Daddy? I've missed you so much," said Molly, blinking back tears.

The father turned toward Karen. "Karen, I don't know if I can do this."

"It's up to you, Jeff. You suggested telling her the truth."

Jeff's face was a mixture of pain and emptiness as he came back to Molly's bedside. "Molly, there's something I need to tell you."

"What, Daddy? Is it about Adam? Won't they let him come see me?"

"No, dear. Adam is fine."

Molly wrinkled her forehead but said nothing. All that mattered to her was that her daddy was next to her. He would take care of her and make sure she got better.

"It's about the man that hit you and mommy," he said.

"Did the police get him?" quipped Molly. "I hope they put him in jail and never, ever let him out again."

"Sweetheart," interrupted Karen, "listen to your father."

"He made it so I couldn't go to soccer practice. I'd like Rex to bite him. Then he'd see how it feels to be in the hospital."

Jeff turned away, but Karen reached out for his hand.

"I can't do it," he whispered. Karen pulled on his arm, and their eyes met for just a moment. Then Jeff walked over to the end of Molly's bed and stared straight at her.

She had never seen him look so sad in her entire life. "Daddy, are you all right?"

"Molly, the man in the car who hit you…was me."

☙

What impact does an affair have on those we love? This fictional story is based on a young girl's moving letter to her straying father contained in John Trent's and Gary Smalley's outstanding book, *The Language of Love*. She likened his adulterous affair to an auto accident that left her, her brother, and her mother all badly bruised and wounded. She's correct. Adultery is a collision of trust relationships that injures and scars everyone involved.[1]

How do you heal broken hearts after such a human cataclysm? What if your spouse asks for forgiveness? What if you want to try to save the marriage and keep the family intact? It's then one of the most difficult journeys in life begins—the journey of forgiveness, rebuilding trust, and banishing the "other" woman or man from your life forever.

Can it be done? Yes, but not easily, not quickly, and not without cost.

But is it worth the effort?

The only way to answer that question is to ask ourselves several other questions. How valuable is it to mend a child's broken heart? How important is it to keep a family together? How precious to God are the promises we made before him and others when we married?

Please let me underscore something. I am not encouraging spouses who have been the victims of their partners' infidelity to take the other person back without repentance and significant changes. The violation of the relationship caused by adultery is so severe that Jesus allowed it as grounds for divorce, as found in Matthew 19:1–12.

But if after the anguish of an affair both partners want to save the marriage, what can be done? While the answer is in one sense quite dependent upon circumstances, three general principles need to be followed.

There must be sincere repentance.

We have several mistaken ideas about repentance in our culture. It is not simply saying, "I'm sorry." The fact that someone says he regrets holding up a bank is no indication he won't put on a ski mask and head for another savings and loan his first day out of jail. *Sorry* may simply mean he wishes he didn't have to face the consequences of his actions.

Nor is repentance acting depressed about our actions. There are rows of glum inmates in state prisons and county jails, but statistics tell us as many as 50 percent of them will be back there again some day. An emotional mood or state of mind doesn't prove a change of heart.

If saying "I'm sorry" isn't enough, if acting sad isn't adequate, and if even doing nice things doesn't erase the past, how do we show genuine repentance? For the answer we have to turn to the Scriptures. The New Testament word for *repentance* means "to undergo a change in frame of mind and feeling, to make a change of principle and practice, to reform by turning away from one's sins."

Genuine repentance in the case of adultery requires the offending spouse to undergo a radical change of practice and perspective. He or she cannot offer excuses such as "You weren't meeting my needs," "I was bored and needed some fun," or "It was only a one-night stand." The person needs to come to the point of saying, "What I did was inexcusable. It was selfish. It was foolish. It was egocentric. All I cared about was my own self-centered desires. I violated the most basic promise of our relationship for no good reason whatsoever." When someone reaches that point and appears to be genuine, the process of repentance has begun.

Consider the story of the Prodigal Son. This young man squandered his father's wealth, lived in open fornication with prostitutes, and destroyed the family name. When he decided to seek reconciliation with his father, he headed home. As soon as he saw his father, the first words out of his mouth were "Father, I have sinned against heaven and against you. I am no longer worthy to be called your son" (Luke 15:21).

He could have said, "Listen, Dad, all those stories about my getting high and running with the babes are so much hype. Besides, you were a controlling father, and I was only acting out my pain. I'm willing to forget this ever happened."

Genuine repentance never seeks to justify wrong actions; rather it owns the selfishness, the true sinfulness, and the real pain our behavior has caused others. Don't settle for anything less than a genuine change in the frame of mind and feelings.

Genuine repentance also involves a change of outlook on the world. For example, people who repent of adultery now recognize that meeting their own needs, desires, and fantasies is not what marriage is all about. They reorient their entire world-view from a self-centered one to a God-centered and spouse-centered perspective. They now realize that all the little lies, all the sneaking around, and all the irresponsible sexual encounters were symptoms of a diseased, sinful philosophy of life.

The Apostle Paul lived in a world of such decadence, sensuality, and indulgence it would make shop owners in Times Square squeamish. He described the values of his day by saying, "Their destiny is destruction, their god is their stomach, and their glory is in their shame" (Philippians 3:19). We live in a remarkably similar world.

Recently the twenty-fifth anniversary of the Woodstock rock concert was held in New York. Aging baby boomers returned to hear aging rock stars play aging songs from the sixties. Because it rained most of the weekend, the world mainly saw men and women in their thirties and forties covered with mud. Somehow it was a metaphor for those in the group who had spent their lives reveling in drugs, sex, and music. The mud that caked their bodies conveyed just how much some of them had lived for and worshiped the values of this world.

The final element of genuine repentance is a change of behavior. Spouses who have repented of infidelity no longer let their eyes wander at the office. They don't spend time teasing and flirting with others. They certainly don't call or arrange to meet their former lovers again for lunch.

Instead, they plan time alone with their spouses. When they find temptation tugging, they pick up the phone and call their husbands or wives. They practice learning their spouses' needs, such as affection or companionship, and plan creative ways to meet them. They throw away any gift, token, or item that emotionally links them to their past affairs.

In other words, they actually start living differently. Until this type of genuine repentance is obvious, I would be cautious about believing a person has changed. While no one could accomplish all these things overnight, the sense of progress must be there.

There must be a slow process of rebuilding trust.

During the height of the Cold War in the 1980s, when leaders in the Soviet Union were trying to negotiate a reduction in nuclear arms with the United States, President Reagan often quoted a Russian proverb: "Trust, but verify."

On one occasion he stood next to General Secretary Gorbachev, then leader of the Soviet Union, and quoted this proverb. The Russian leader got visibly upset and interrupted him. "Why do you always say that?"

Always the gentleman, President Reagan smiled at him and replied, "Because it's true."

That same proverb will equally serve married couples who are recovering from an affair. "Trust, but verify."

Even though a spouse appears to have undergone genuine repentance, he or she must undergo the painstaking process of earning back trust. Adultery is a class one felony, not a petty misdemeanor, when it comes to trust. It is fraud, deceit, and betrayal at the deepest levels of a relationship.

So how does a couple rebuild trust? It begins with accountability. Dr. Willard Harley suggests the offending spouse draw up a daily time log, broken into fifteen-minute increments. The husband or wife who strayed fills in where he or she will be each of those fifteen-minute segments of the day, complete with phone numbers. The other spouse is then given the prerogative to call or drop in at any time of the day, as often as desired.

Such cautious rebuilding makes sense. To immediately give back the keys to the bank to an employee who embezzled $250,000 would be an act of foolishness, not love or generosity. In the same way, to place complete trust in a husband or wife without requiring that partner to prove faithful over time is unwise.

I'm not suggesting people throw their spouses' sins back in their faces on a daily basis. People who for years continually humiliate and punish their mates for one sexual failure are exercising revenge and degradation, not love and trust building.

But it's fair to set boundaries. For example, if a wife chooses to take back a husband who repents and wants to rebuild trust, she could offer this warning: "I believe you may be sincere in your assurance that you will never be unfaithful to me again. However, it will take time for me to see whether or not you are telling the truth. You need to know that if you are ever unfaithful to me again, you will have ended this marriage. I will file for divorce, and there will be no opportunity for reconciliation."

Is that too harsh? It may be the only way to save a marriage. Dr. James Dobson, author of *Love Must Be Tough,* points out that only when we demonstrate tough love in the face of infidelity can respect be reintroduced into a relationship. And respect is the essential ingredient of re-creating love.

Regardless of the particular circumstances of the adultery, one fact is indisputable—the unfaithful spouse committed an ultimate act of disrespect. For the marriage to have any chance of surviving, new boundaries must be drawn and enforced. If the offending spouse knows that another episode of adultery will not be tolerated, it will likely engender a healthy deference for the mate's boundaries. That, according to Dobson, is often the key to reawakening love in the marriage.

I have seen the faces of spouses whose mates have cheated, asked forgiveness, and then have gone out and done the same thing two, three, and four more times. The resulting pain and grief for the innocent spouse are impossible to describe. They thought they were doing the right thing to keep taking their mates back, but because they failed to draw and enforce boundaries, they lost their mates' respect. Unwittingly they may have even made it easier for them to stray again.

One of the most poignant sights of this decade was the televised funeral of Richard Nixon. A man who had left office in disgrace in 1974 for betraying the trust of the American people was buried with full honors with five U. S. presidents in attendance.

For over two decades Nixon had worked quietly to re-establish the trust he had so foolishly forfeited while in office. He wrote books, gave speeches, and quietly advised sitting presidents on foreign policy. By the end of his life, both friends and foes,

Democrats and Republicans, admitted he had won back the respect of the American people. Even his archrival, George McGovern, attended his funeral and wept.

For couples working to heal broken trust, his example is worthwhile. Time, faithfulness, and a desire to be believed again are required.

There must be an understanding of the cost of forgiveness.

I once heard a shock talk show host on a Chicago radio station pose the question to listeners, "If your spouse committed adultery, could you forgive and forget it happened?" Most of the callers responded, "I could probably forgive him [or her], but I doubt I could ever forget it." "Then you can't forgive them!" he would shout back. "Unless you forget, you haven't forgiven."

He was badly mistaken. Forgiveness doesn't imply we hypnotize ourselves or delete large sections of our lives from our memory. That's unrealistic, if not impossible. Forgiveness is not forgetting that something painful was done to us; it's releasing the other person from the moral debt he or she owes us.

Too often we trivialize forgiveness. Someone hurts us, apologizes, and we respond by saying, "No big deal." Minimizing what the other person did is not forgiveness. That's denial. Rather, forgiveness is making the costly decision to bear the injustice without requiring the other person to remain in our moral debt.

When spouses commit adultery, they have broken the most sacred pledge they have ever made to another human being. The penalty for that breach of contract is the right to cancel the agreement altogether. The offended party is no longer obligated to stay in the relationship. Adultery has in essence made the terms of the marriage covenant null and void.

So if people choose to forgive their spouses, they are taking on themselves the consequences of their mates' behavior without requiring payment for it. That's costly. That's difficult. That's the nature of forgiveness. That's exactly what Jesus Christ did for us on the cross: "He himself bore our sins in his body on the tree, so that we might die to sins and live for righteousness; by his wounds you have been healed" (1 Peter 2:24).

Several years ago a man who had been a frequent speaker, a successful author, and a role model committed adultery. Yet, throughout the humiliation and pain of the ordeal, his wife chose to forgive him. She appeared in public by his side. She faced the people he had disappointed by his side. She even went on radio with him as he explained his mistakes. It was an extremely difficult thing to do. It was his sin, not hers, but she acted as if it were hers as well. She was willing to bear the consequences of what he had done to her and others. Their marriage survived, and a new example of grace was given to the world.

CONCLUSION

Molly's father had been gone ever since the accident. Each night she prayed he'd come home.

Molly cautiously stepped off the school bus. It was her second week back at school. She was now strong enough to walk home from the corner without her mother's help. She said goodbye to Jennifer, her next door neighbor, as they split up on the sidewalk.

"Let's play after supper," suggested Jennifer.

"Mom says I still have to rest at night," said Molly. "It helps my headaches to go away."

"Okay, see you tomorrow," came the reply.

Molly turned toward her driveway and stopped. A new, metallic green car was parked there. "It can't be," she said out loud.

She dropped her backpack on the sidewalk and started to walk fast, then run toward the door. By the time she reached the door, her heart was racing. Holding on to the knob, she pushed the door open. The dog met her and jumped up. "Mom, are you home?"

"I'm here, sweetheart," Karen said.

Molly walked into the living room and was met by two large suitcases. She looked up, and there on the couch, holding hands, were her mom and dad.

Chapter Thirteen

A MODEST PROPOSAL TO REKINDLE YOUR LOVE LIFE

I was leaving the expressway one evening when a billboard caught my attention. A question was emblazoned there in huge, blue letters: "Diane, will you marry me?" I could only wonder how many Dianes had rushed home, dialed their unsuspecting boyfriends, and shouted, "Yes!"

The billboard was clever and romantic, but it asked the wrong question. In fact, fifteen years ago when I asked Cheryl if she would marry me, I missed the point as well. Instead of posing the question "Will you marry me?" I should have asked, "Will you be married to me?"

The difference is more than semantic. Essentially the first question only asks, "Will you set a date, go through a ceremony, and sign a certificate with me?" The second asks, "Will you make a lifetime commitment to keep romance alive, to bear my burdens, to spend time together in the Bible, to show respect to me in front of others, and to work hard at keeping my dreams alive?"

That's a mouthful when you're down on one knee, but it comes closer to describing what a vital, growing marriage requires. If you're like me and asked—or answered—the wrong question, the good news is it's not too late to propose again, whether you're the husband or the wife. The following five questions make a great second proposal.

1. Will you keep romance alive in our relationship for a lifetime?

Women are often more interested in keeping romance alive than men are. During courtship a great deal of a man's enthusiasm for buying flowers, writing thoughtful notes, and finding romantic places to eat is fueled by pent-up sexual energy. Once that sexual need is met in marriage, a husband's efforts to romance his wife may begin to feel like work.

A friend of my wife once tried to attract her husband's attention after dinner by walking into the room wearing nothing but a negligee. Her husband yawned and went back to the book he was reading. He felt their ongoing sexual relationship was meeting his needs, and that was all the "romance" he wanted.

That's why your second marriage proposal should include a lifelong commitment to keep romance alive. The adage is true: "If you want to feel romantic, act romantic." Writing thoughtful notes, spending time in deep conversation, and enjoying quiet walks together all build intimacy. The objective is not just sexual intimacy, but emotional, relational, and spiritual intimacy as well.

As I make the effort to keep romance alive in my marriage, feelings of closeness and attraction are rekindled. Those feelings may be less intense than they were during my bachelor days, but fifteen years later, they are certainly more fulfilling.

2. Will you bear my burdens as I carry yours for a lifetime?

It's too bad that when I asked Cheryl to marry me, I didn't ask for the privilege of shouldering her sorrows and difficulties. I should have, because bearing each other's burdens is a great part of what it means to be married.

When Cheryl was pregnant with our first child, she became terribly ill and weak. As she was hospitalized, I stayed with her, held her hand, and waited with her for the suffering to pass. Shortly after our first son was born, her uncle was killed in a collision just minutes after dropping Cheryl and the baby off. I stood by her in her grief.

Likewise, when I was laid off from my job, Cheryl offered comfort and support. Once, when I appeared to be facing a debilitating illness, she promised she'd stay right by my side.

Neither of us bargained for such pain and difficulties the day we announced our engagement. But our willingness to bear one another's burdens has been one of the most important and meaningful experiences of our marriage. Paul encourages us in Galatians 6:2 to "carry each other's burdens, and in this way you will fulfill the law of Christ." The law he refers to is the law of love, and burden bearing is at the very heart of marriage.

3. Will you promise to spend time with me in the Bible?

Each of us should be reading the Bible regularly on our own, of course, but there is something uniquely powerful in reading the Bible to one another. In Ephesians, Paul uses the metaphor of "bathing" one another in the truth, wisdom, and comfort of the Scriptures. Over time the pressures and problems of life take the luster off our souls. God's Word can restore a sense of freshness, purity, and vitality.

The intent, however, is not to misuse Scripture as a chisel to remake our spouses into our own images or as a spiritual paddle to punish our mates for perceived imperfections and misbehavior.

When a friend of mine was invited to lead three couples in a Bible study on marriage, he quickly discovered the real agenda of the woman who had organized the study. She wanted a group setting where she could pressure her husband to become a "new and improved" spouse. Not surprisingly, it was a long and miserable ten weeks of "sharing."

That's not what I'm advocating. Sharing meaningful passages with one another, finding appropriate verses to deal with your spouse's pain, and soothing a frustrated mind and soul with words of assurance are gifts you can give each other through God's Word.

4. Will you treat me with respect in front of your friends and family members as I do the same for you?

Cheryl and I stayed one night in a home where the tension between the husband and wife was like an August atmospheric inversion. We could hardly breathe. The next morning we got up, packed our things, and politely excused ourselves from the danger zone.

Honoring one another before the world is nothing more than simple courtesy. But it involves restraining our emotions, swallowing hurtful words before they leave our mouths, and remembering that public humiliation leaves lifelong scars. Honor isn't simply the absence of put-downs; it's also the presence of affirmation and respect. It's being willing to get up and excuse ourselves from a meeting because our spouse dropped by the office or is on the phone.

When I worked in an administrative setting, I left word with the receptionist that my wife should always be put through, regardless of what I was doing. It was a sign of respect. Likewise,

Cheryl has always refused to criticize me to friends. She's been known to steer the conversation in another direction rather than have the husbands for dessert.

Proverbs, chapter 31, advises husbands, "Give her the reward she has earned, and let her works bring her praise at the city gate." The same could be said for wives honoring their husbands.

If your marriage is suffering from respect-impairment, let me suggest you correct the problem through praise and affirmation, particularly in front of business associates, friends, and family. The rehabilitation of your love for one another will be nothing less than a miracle.

5. *Will you work hard at keeping my dreams alive?*

The pressures of dealing with high mortgage payments, car repairs, and chicken pox can little by little wear us down. If we're not careful, we can end up so depleted by survival-fatigue that we allow our aspirations and visions to quietly die.

My wife graduated from college and went on to earn a master's degree. Yet she has given herself to the incredible demands of raising four children. To help preserve her time for herself, I bought her a membership in a local health club as a birthday gift. It gives her time to exercise, read, and reflect on her priorities for that day.

Though her primary desire was to be a loving wife and mother, I knew she had other aspirations as well for the future. So during those particularly hard early years, I tried to say to her over and over, "I want to keep your other dreams alive as well." Today she lends invaluable ideas and insights to the nonprofit ministry we established together, and we find mutual fulfillment in our roles as parents and co-workers.

Paul gives us practical advice on dream-preservation in Philippians 2:4: "Each of you should look not only to your own interests, but also to the interests of others."

CONCLUSION

I'm glad it's not too late to propose to my wife again. The first time was during the evening news. This time I think I'll find a more appropriate setting. More importantly, this time I'll ask the right questions.[1]

NOTES

Chapter 1: Who's Having the Best Sex Anyhow?

1. Robert Michael et al., *Sex in America: A Definitive Survey* (Boston: Little, Brown and Company, 1994), 1, 13-14.

2. Ibid., 116.

3. Ibid., 112.

4. Ibid., 128-29.

5. Ibid., 113.

6. Garrison Keillor, "It's Good Old Monogamy that's Really Sexy," *Time,* 17 October 1994, 71.

7. Michael, *Sex in America,* 1.

8. Erma Bombeck, "Just Who Answers These Polls Anyway?" *Arlington Heights Daily Herald,* 1 November 1994.

Chapter 3: Good Sex Begins in the Bible

1. Michael, *Sex in America,* 192–94.

2. Bill Farrel et al., *Pure Pleasure: Making Your Marriage a Great Affair* (Downers Grove, Ill.: InterVarsity Press, 1994), 120–21.

3. Michael, *Sex in America,* 125.

4. Ibid., 127-30.

Chapter 4: Aren't My Needs Your Needs?

1. Willard Harley, *His Needs, Her Needs: Building an Affair Proof Marriage* (Grand Rapids: Fleming H. Revell, 1986), 11.

2. Ibid., 10–11.

3. Michael, *Sex in America,* 156.

4. Ibid., 93.

5. Lois Leiderman Davitz, Ph.D., "Why Men Divorce," *McCall's* (March 1987): 26.

6. Harley, *His Needs, Her Needs,* 29.

7. Michael, *Sex in America,* 116.

8. Davitz, "Why Men Divorce," 26.

9. Jimmy Evans, *Marriage on the Rock* (New York: McCrecken Press, 1994).

Chapter 5: Time Will Let You

1. Keillor, "Good Old Monogamy," 71.

2. Nathan Hatch, "The Gift of Brokenness: The Outrageously Fruitful Ministry of My Father," *Christianity Today*, 14 November 1994, 34.

3. Farrel, *Pure Pleasure*, 191.

4. Michael, *Sex in America*, 125.

Chapter 6: Keep the Grease Pit Drained

1. Robert Hemfelt, Paul Meier, and Frank Minirth, *Love Is a Choice* (Nashville: Thomas Nelson, 1989).

2. Norman Shawchuck, *How to Manage Conflict in the Church: Understanding and Managing Conflict* (Indianapolis: Spiritual Growth Resources, 1983), 36.

3. Shawchuck, *How to Manage Conflict*, 46–47.

4. James Dobson, *Love Must Be Tough* (Waco: Word Books, 1983), 151–53.

Chapter 7: What You Do When No One Is Watching

1. Frank Pittman, *Private Lies: Infidelity and the Betrayal of Intimacy* (New York: Norton, 1989), 89, quoted in "Secrets of Staying Together," *Reader's Digest*, March 1989, 151–54.

2. William Frey, "Really Good Sex" *Christianity Today*, 19 August 1991, 12.

3. "The War Within: An Anatomy of Lust," *Leadership Journal* 3, no. 4 (Fall 1982), 33.

4. Bob Moeller, "What if Beer Ads Lasted Longer than 30 Seconds?" *Focus on the Family*, January 1994, 11.

5. "I Loved You Once in Silence," from *Camelot*, Warner Brothers Records, 1967.

Chapter 8: Divorce Is the Problem, Not the Solution

1. "The Next Mrs. Windsor?" *Time*, 23 January 1995, 63.

2. Michael, *Sex in America*, 112.

3. Ibid., 5.

4. Ibid., 84–85.

5. Ibid., 87.

6. Lawrence Kurdek, "The Relations between Well-being and Divorce History, Availability of a Proximate Adult, and Gender," *Journal of Marriage and the Family* 53 (February 1991): 71–78. See also Alan Booth and John Edwards, "Starting Over: Why Remarriages are More Unstable," *Journal of Family Issues* 13 (June 1992): 179–94.

7. Leslie Morgan, "Economic Well-being Following Marital Termination: A Comparison of Widowed and Divorced Women," *Journal of Family Issues* 10 (March 1989): 86–101.

Chapter 9: How to Reconnect a Disconnected Sex Life

1. Jim Dethmer, "The Best Kept Secret About Sex," *The Christian Reader* (July/August 1994): 28.

2. "I Needed to Have an Affair," *Ladies Home Journal,* March 1992, 96.

3. Ibid., 95–96.

4. Bill Hybels and Rob Wilkins, *Tender Love: God's Gift of Sexual Intimacy* (Chicago: Moody Press, 1993): 138–39.

5. David A. Seamands, *Healing for Damaged Emotions: Recovering from the Memories that Cause Our Pain* (Wheaton, Ill.: Victor Books, 1981), 30-31.

Chapter 10: The Trial Was an Error

1. Michael, *Sex in America,* 96–97, 99.

2. Ibid., 103–104.

3. Ibid., 103.

4. Ibid.

5. Roger Hillerstrom, *Intimate Deception: Escaping the Trap of Sexual Impurity* (Portland, Ore.: Multnomah Books, 1989), 43.

6. *New Research: The Family in America* (Rockford, Ill.: The Rockford Institute Center on the Family in America, December 1987), 1, quoted in *Intimate Deception,* 28.

7. Elizabeth Thomas and Ugo Collela, "Cohabitation and Marital Stability: Quality or Commitment," *Journal of Marriage and the Family* 54, no. 2 (May 1992): 759-67.

8. Michael, *Sex in America,* 224–25.

9. Hillerstrom, *Intimate Deception,* 145–46.

10. Ibid., 32–33.

11. Donald Joy, *Bonding: Relationships in the Image of God* (Waco, Tex.: Word Books, 1985), 10-11.

Chapter 11: Recovering from Visual Adultery

1. Michael, *Sex in America,* 157.

2. "The War Within," 30-43.

3. Dolf Zillman and Jennings Bryant, "The Effect of Prolonged Consumption of Pornography on Family Values," *Journal of Family Issues* 9, no. 4 (December 1988): 518-44.

4. Kathryn Casey, "Women and Pornography," *Ladies Home Journal,* August 1992, 117, 175.

5. Ibid., 176.

6. Ibid., 177.

7. Joy, *Bonding,* 10-11.

8. Hal B. Schell, Gary Sweeten, with Betty Reid, "Freeing the Sexually Addicted," *Leadership Journal* 10, no. 4 (Fall 1984): 58.

9. Ibid., 59.

Chapter 12: Can You Heal a Broken Heart?

1. Gary Smalley and John Trent, *The Language of Love* (Colorado Springs: Focus on the Family, 1994).

Chapter 13: A Modest Proposal to Rekindle Your Love Life

1. Robert Moeller, "What Did You Really Promise When You Said, 'I Do'?" *Marriage Partnership,* Summer 1993, 20–22.